How to Get Rich in Central Ohio Real Estate

What You Need to Know, Get, and Do to Build a Wildly Successful Real Estate Investing Business Starting from Scratch

By Vena Jones-Cox
Author, Lecturer, Real Estate Goddess
TheRealEstateGoddess.com

Table of Contents

My Life in Real Estate

My name is Vena, and I'm a real estate addict.

After a short-lived and miserable[1] career in corporate America, I discovered that, at the age of 23, with a nearly-useless but very-expensive degree in sociology, I was apparently unemployable.

I disliked everything about having a "job", from the dress code to the commute to those silly policies about showing up on time. And my bosses disliked everything about me, from my smart mouth to my red/violet hair to my unwillingness to show up early and stay late.

So, with $70,000 in credit card and student loan debt and nothing better to do, I joined my family's real estate business in 1989.

My father was a dyed-in-the-wool "Mom and Pop" landlord, by which I mean that he could—and would—fix a leaky boiler pipe with rubber bands, flattened aluminum cans, and Bond-O. When the phone rang at 11:29 p.m., he'd answer it in case it was a tenant reporting a roof leak. And if it was, he'd jump in his car and be out until 2 a.m. putting a tarp on the roof in the dark and the rain. He was worth millions on paper, but our family "vacations" consisted largely of going to places where we had family we could stay with, because, and I quote, "Money is for investing, not spending".

This was not a philosophy (or lifestyle) that tends to inspire a 23 year old.

In fact, I considered this new job—which had the advantage of allowing me to dress as I pleased and backtalk the boss, but the disadvantage of paying just $18,000 a year[2]--something to do to pay the bills until I figured out what I wanted to do with my life

---

[1]   For both myself and my employer
[2]   With the bonus, according to my father "Inheriting all this money you're making me"

1

So for two years, I treaded water, building my father's estate, learning the ropes of the rental business, dreaming of the day that I'd find a career that would make me anxious to jump out of bed in the morning and get to work.

Then, something happened that changed my view of real estate—and my life—forever. In 90 minutes, I was transformed from real estate agnostic ("Yeah, they say it's a great way to have a great lifestyle, but I'll believe it when I see it") to real estate addict.

That thing was simple: **I attended a meeting of my local real estate investor's association**. The speaker that evening was an out-of-town expert who claimed that it was possible to make money in real estate WITHOUT dealing with tenants and their intoxicated midnight service requests. In fact, he said that I could earn my entire year's salary in about 4 deals by "Quick Turning" them—assigning purchase contracts to other investors for a one-time cash payment, or in 2 deals a year by "Flipping" them—fixing them up and selling them to homeowners for a $10,000-$15,000 profit

I was stunned.

How could such a thing exist, and I didn't know about it? Was this guy full of it? Was this even legal? Five THOUSAND dollars[3] from a single deal, with no tenants, toilets, going to the bank on bended knee and begging for a loan?

Now THAT was something I could get excited about.

So, the next day at work, I called a meeting with my father to enlighten him about this new strategy this guy had invented, and how it was going to transform our[4] business overnight.

---

[3] Remember, this was in the early '90s. $5,000 on a wholesale deal was a LOT of money in the early 90's.

[4] If you've ever worked in a family business, you know that it's "our" business when YOU'RE the one being asked to set the mousetraps. When you're asking for a bigger share of the profits, it s HIS business.

His response? "Oh, you mean that quick-flippin [5]? I know about that. But we're not gonna do it, because the guy you sell it to makes all the money and the gubment[6] takes away half of it in taxes, anyway[7]."

There was no convincing him to do these cash-producing strategies—and no convincing him to let me do it on the side. So I put $3,000 on a credit card, drove to Chicago to attend a 3-day bootcamp about how to flip houses, came home, quit my job[8], and started my own business.

And I've never, ever, looked back.

Much has happened since that day in 1992.

I eventually became the president of that local real estate association, and then the Ohio Real Estate Investors Association, and then the National Real Estate Investors Association, and then I started the Central Ohio Real Estate Entrepreneurs (COREE) for good measure.

I became a licensed broker. I created my own home study course for new investors, and then another for people who wanted to learn to wholesale properties, and then one for people who wanted to lease/option, then another on marketing, and one on creative buying, and one on negotiation, and one on real estate business systems.

I've taught literally thousands of people how to get rich in real estate, and coached hundreds more one-on-one to build full-time real estate businesses. I've been the out-of-town expert at more than 200 associations and conventions across the U.S. and Canada. I've testified

---

[5] My dad was from Altus, Oklahoma

[6] And could never quite pronounce government, or library, despite having a degree in chemical engineering and having spent 40 years in the Midwest.

[7] Did I mention that dyed-in-the-wool landlords are violently allergic to paying taxes?

[8] A move that still, to this day, generates semi-hostile conversation around the holiday dinner table

at the Cato Institute[9] about the detrimental effects of government interference on the housing industry.

And, in an abnormal move for a real estate 'guru', I've continued to buy, and sell, and rent, and finance, and fix, and manage properties—and to learn new and better and more efficient ways to do these things—year in and year out.

I've dealt in investment real estate in "up" markets and "down". I've long since lost count of the number of houses I've owned or wholesaled, but I can tell you the number is upwards of 800 as of this writing. I've done my 10,000 hours. I know what works and what doesn't, and I stay on top of the fast-moving market not just because I teach other people how to get rich in real estate, but because I make the vast majority of my income by buying, selling, and renting it.

But most importantly, I adore what I do.

Not every bit of it, of course—like any business person, I have my share of unpleasant decisions to make and grinding tasks to get through. But I do wake up every morning anxious to get to work, looking forward to what the day will bring, and thrilled to be able to take advantage of the financial independence that real estate investing has brought into my life.

That's what I want for you, too. And that's why I've written this book—to get you off to the right start investing in real estate in your own back yard.

---

[9]   Back when it was a cool libertarian think tank rather than a crazy right-wing one

INTRODUCTION:

Why Central Ohio Real Estate Rocks

It always amazes me when real estate wannabes tell me that they want to invest in, or wholesale, or retail, properties in a city hundreds or thousands of miles from where they live.

"I heard Memphis is a great rental market, so I'm going to buy some rentals there", they'll say. Or, "Texas has such a great economy—I want to flip houses in Austin". Or, "Look at the money those guys on T.V. are making retailing houses in San Diego! I'm going to look for some houses (and contractors, and suppliers) there."

This "grass is greener" syndrome might even make sense in markets that are on the extreme edges of housing affordability, or of regulatory aggressiveness. For instance, it's extremely difficult on the coast of southern California to find a property that makes sense as a rental. Prices are too high, and rents too low as a percentage of the value of the property, to generate an acceptable return on investment[10]. Or, to put that in English, you can buy 3 houses in Columbus, Ohio for the same price as one in San Diego, and get twice the cash flo . And Texas, where lease/options and contracts for deed are extremely heavily regulated, those strategies are better practiced on out-of-state properties.

---

[10] Unless, as one SoCal student told me recently, your real goal is to ride the wacky California real estate wave to the top and double your money in 5-7 years. If it works, the month-over-month losses are more than made up for by the frenzy-driven appreciation. The problem, of course, is that, as in the mighty Pacific, those big waves tend to crash.

5

But the bottom line is that most real estate[11] is not like other "investments", in the sense that you do some online research, decide if it's a good deal, invest your money, and never think about your asset except when the check comes each month, or quarter, or year. In fact, for most people who are starting with little in the way of money or credit, real estate "investing" isn't investing at all—it's a business that happens to use houses/apartments/mobile homes/commercial properties/whatever as inventory.

In fact, you'll find that most of your rich, successful, high-income Central Ohio colleagues will tell you that they (or, later in their careers, someone in their company that they've trained) has been into every single solitary property they've ever bought or sold. They've driven the neighborhood. They've looked at the roof and the foundation and the kitchen and the bath and all of the other important features of the property IN PERSON. They've smelled the smells. They've looked at the "comparable sales", in the field, to make sure that those properties were, in fact, comparable in size and appearance and location.

In other words, one of the secrets of their—and your—success is being "hands on" in their evaluations of their properties BEFORE they bought them.

And this is a whole lot easier when you're in Westerville and your proposed rental is in Grove City than it is when you're in Upper Arlington and you're trying to buy a tax lien in Houston.

Luckily, here in Central Ohio, we have a unique combination of factors that make real estate—whether you intend to buy and hold, buy and sell, or wholesale, or buy mortgages, or all of the above—an extremely good business to be in. It's not perfect, but it's about as close to perfect as any market I've ever seen—and I've seen a lot of them.

---

[11] Yes, there are such things as truly passive investments involving real estate. If this seems more up your alley than actual work, see page 104 for how to learn more about them.

In fact, it might be easier *for the average person* to get rich in Central Ohio real estate than it is in much of the rest of the United States, and here's why:

Our economy is built on stable ground. Unlike the dying "rust belt" cities in Ohio, which depended largely on fast-disappearing manufacturing jobs to employ their citizens, Central Ohio's economy is based in the academic, financial, health, and, of course, ever-expanding government sectors. Since it's unlikely these 21st century services businesses[12] will be shipped overseas anytime soon, the Greater Columbus area and surrounding communities will continue to attract new workers—and therefore, new renters and buyers—for the foreseeable future.

Our real estate is affordable. With median house prices in the $100,000-$130,000 range depending on the county, and some individual neighborhoods with properties selling for under $40,000 on average, we live in one of the most affordable markets in the U.S.

Although "median price" means less to you as an educated investor (because you'll always pay less for a property than it's actually worth, and rarely use bank financing to buy a property), it means a LOT to you as a seller, and to the strength of the local housing market as a whole.

Affordability is not just a function of house prices, of course, but also of median household income. The National Association of Realtors™ creates an annual affordability index that measures these factors; an affordability index of 100 means that the family earning exactly the median income for the area can exactly afford the median priced house for the area at current conventional mortgage rates and terms. A higher affordability index number means that more people can afford the median priced house. A lower affordability index means that less than 50% of the local populace can buy.

---

[12]   Or, God forbid, the Buckeyes

Central Ohio's affordability index is 286.1. San Jose California's is 86.2. Remind me, where would you rather be fixing and selling houses, again?

We have a wide variety of housing stock within a relatively small geographic area. Whatever type of property, neighborhood, or strategy you'd love to specialize in, you'll probably find it within 20 miles of your front door.

Love the idea of historic rehabs? There are plenty of architecturally-interesting turn-of-the-century row houses in Columbus's German Village[13] that will undoubtedly get your blood pumping.

Want to own high-cash-flo , low-end rentals? Check out any of the city's "first suburbs" surrounding downtown.

Like the idea of rural properties that sell like hotcakes on contract for deed? Head out to Madison, Union, or Pickaway Counties—you'll also find your mobile homes and manufactured homes out there, if that's your preference.

And, of course there are endless neighborhoods and suburbs with houses of all sizes, ages, and price ranges available for you to buy and rent or buy and sell.

Speaking of buying and renting, we have one of the lowest purchase-price-to-rent ratios in the country—which means incredibly high returns on your investment dollar. In more expensive markets in the U.S., it's often the case that what a property will rent for is .75% or less of the value of the property. For instance, in Los Angeles, where a bread-and-butter single family home in a first-time homebuyer area might sell for $250,000, that property will only rent for $1,500 per month, or .6% of the value of the house. In Central Ohio, that same property is only worth $100,000—and will rent for $1,000 a month, or 1% of the value of the property.

---

[13] Though, ironically, no German architecture whatsoever.

In our urban areas, the numbers become even better for the landlord: according to Zillow.com, the average sale price for a home in the Columbus neighborhood of Linden was $37,000 and the average rent was $575 a month—or 1.5% of the value—in 2012.

We have great resources for finding deals—and finding property values. In many parts of the country, including neighboring Kentucky and Indiana, public records are very difficult to access. This makes it tough to even determine what houses are selling for in a particular area without paying for expensive services or becoming a real estate agent.

Here in Ohio, we're fortunate to have easy—usually online—access to sale prices of homes (see www.FranklinCountyAuditor.org for an great example). What's more, it's easy to access lists of potentially motivated sellers, including owners who are in foreclosure, behind on property taxes, who have inherited properties, and many more. Ask real estate entrepreneurs in other states and they'll tell you that this easy availability of ownership and legal information is a huge advantage to us in Central Ohio.

A relatively favorable regulatory environment. Yes, I know, the eviction courts are tenant-friendly, and the process takes too long, and foreclosures go on forever and ever here.

But compared to other places in the U.S., we have fairly friendly laws here in Central Ohio—laws that don't make it difficult or impossible to make money in real estate.

For instance, did you know that in Maryland, a law called PHIFA makes it possible for you to go to jail simply for negotiating to buy the home of a homeowner in foreclosure? Or that, in Texas, selling on lease/option is so restricted that it's practically never done? Or that an eviction in New York can take up to a year? Or that Section 8 voucher holders are a protected class in parts of Illinois—you can't refuse to rent to those tenants and jump through all of Section 8's hoops without breaking the law?

9

Yep, we have it pretty good here—and it's largely due to a 30 year old state association called the Ohio Real Estate Investor's Association, which is one of just 5 such associations in the entire U.S. It has been tracking and lobbying against anti-investor laws for decades, which is why those of us who invest here in Ohio aren't subject to such heinous, business-ending rules and regulations.

A sharing investor community organized into a strong local and state educational association. This may be the most important advantage that Central Ohio investors have, and it will certainly be the key to YOUR success as a wholesaler, retailer, landlord, and real estate entrepreneur in the area.

Central Ohio's premier local real estate investor's community is Central Ohio Real Estate Entrepreneurs (COREE). At COREE, members at all levels of knowledge and experience meet multiple times each month to learn from experts, share resources, network, do deals, get discounts on products and services, and stay abreast of the ever-changing market.

Not all real estate associations are like COREE—some exist simply to be a source of deals for the group's owners, or to make money selling courses and bootcamps to newbies, or to funnel members into 5-figure mentoring programs.

At COREE, our mission is to provide the education, benefits, and support you need to be a successful, ethical Central Ohio investor, in whatever strategy you choose to follow.

We're the only Columbus-area association that's a member of the business-supporting Ohio Real Estate Investor's Association. We are the local partners of Community Buying Group (CBG), which gives members like you benefits ranging from 7% discounts at Lowes to huge savings at Sherwin Williams, cheap investor-friendly insurance, discounted tenant screenings and tool rental, and much more.

We're also the group where you'll find the most friendly, sharing, open leaders and members—all of whom want to see you reach your goals.

We are local investors that believe that the pie is big enough for all of us, and that an educated, ethical competitor is better than a newly-minted seminar grad who makes mistakes that hurt his sellers, buyers, tenants, and the community.

Plus, it's super-affordable at just $197 per year, with payment plans available, too.

We invite you to join us by attending a free meeting. Download a guest pass at www.CentralOhioREIA.com and we know you'll decide to join.

But for now, let's talk more about what you're going to have to learn, get, and do to get rich in Central Ohio Real Estate.

Why People Get Rich in Central Ohio Real Estate

We all know that real estate is the most effective way around for the average person to build big—like huge, like generation-spanning—wealth. [14]

Andrew Carnegie is credited with saying, "90% of the millionaires in the United States made their money investing in real estate."

Recent success books like Rich Dad, Poor Dad and The Millionaire Next Door tell the story again: rich people get rich partly because they get themselves some extra houses or apartment buildings.

But if you've never played the real estate game, you might not have a super-clear picture of what it's really like. You might figure that you buy a property, do some repairs, put a tenant in it, and wait for the checks to start rolling in–sort of like stock dividends. Or you might imagine that buying bargain properties and reselling them is similar to day trading–all you have to do is call a broker and put the property on the market, and, presto! A buyer comes along the next day.

News flash: real estate investing isn't like the stock market. At all. And this is a good thing.

See, owning and managing, or even flipping, real estate is absolutely, positively more effort than calling your broker and telling him to buy $1,000 worth of this or that. It also requires more education than the typical stock market investor bothers to get about the companies that he invests in.

---

[14] That's you, unless you're going to win the lottery, or invent the next "Pet Rock", or inherit millions from your family. But that wouldn't make you an "average person", would it?

But when it's done right, it's also a whole lot more profitable <u>and more controllable</u> than those sorts of investments.

Ask yourself this: *how many average wage-earners do you know who've gotten rich by investing in the stock market?* Go ahead, count 'em. I'll wait.

That didn't take too long, did it? Because the answer is zero.

But there are tens of thousands of real estate millionaires in the United States who started with nothing more than a dream and a couple of hundred bucks for an association membership, and hundreds of thousands more who've doubled (or more) their incomes by investing in real estate part time.

How is this possible? How can it be that you can start with little or no money and build assets worth 6, 7, or 8 figures in real estate, but not in the stock market?

Well, for one thing, unlike stocks, real estate is highly **leverageable**. This means that you can control a lot of assets with only a little money. You can OWN—as in, have the keys to and the deed to and have all the rights to and income from–a house by putting down 20% of its value and borrowing the rest, right? [15]

Some real estate income is also even more **tax advantaged** than dividend or capital gains income–in fact, if you know what you're doing, you can even sell a property for a massive gain and not pay <u>any</u> capital gains taxes on the profit [16]

At the same time, as we'll discuss in this book, real estate "investment" isn't really investment at all.

---

[15] And that's BEFORE you join COREE and learn how to buy whole houses with $10 down. Most of our members don't use banks to buy, ever—they've been trained in "creative buying" techniques that allow them to buy without all the big down payments, fees, and qualifying. You'll see.
[16] It's called a 1031 tax-deferred exchange, and yes, it's for real.

It's a business, and as such, it's knowledge-intensive. If you're going to be as wealthy and high-income as you can be in real estate, there are certain things you're going to have to decide and learn and do. You may even know some people who chose to "just dive in" and buy a property without having these fundamentals in place, and who learned an expensive and painful lesson as a result.

And here's the silly thing about those ouchy mistakes: given that literally thousands of local folks have already trodden that path and overcome all the pitfalls, there's no reason for you to make the same mistakes.

The purpose of this book is to help you understand, in a general sense, what successful local investors have done to become successful, and how you can take the first, easy steps toward doing the same things.

There's More than One Way to Get Rich in Central Ohio Real Estate

How many different ways can you name to turn a piece of property into cash in your pocket?

If it's just one, or 2, or even 3, you don't have the full picture. And if you don't have the full picture, how are you going to choose the strategy that's best for YOU, in your particular situation and with your particular goals and needs?

The first most important thing you'll do as a budding real estate entrepreneur is take a look at the various "exit strategies"—which is just a way of saying "How you make your properties make money"—and what each one requires and how each one pays you.

Your choice of exit strategy is the most important choice you'll make in the entire course of your real estate career. Why? Because it's the details of your exit strategy that determine practically everything else about what you'll be doing on a day-to-day basis, including:

- What kinds of properties and neighborhoods you'll need to focus on
- How you'll find your great deal
- How you'll figure out what to pay for any particular propert
- Whether you'll need cash or financing to do the deal and, of

so, how much and what kind

- Whether you'll need to have resources to do repairs and, if so, what level of repairs

And even more importantly, the exit strategy you choose will decide what kind of money you make, and when:

- How much profit you'll take home, on average, per dea
- When that profit will come to you (up front, or regularly over time, or at the back end of the deal)
- How that profit will be taxed (at high ordinary income rates or lower rental/interest/capital gains rates)

Many new investors come to COREE confused about the basic exit strategies and what they do. COREE has developed an affordable "Fast Start" program called Express Success that teaches all of the basic strategies and skills in a 6-month series of weekly webinars, and includes coaching for new investors via email. See www.CentralOhioREIA for details.

This is why it's so very, very crucial that you choose the right exit strategies and for the right reasons.

At the end of this chapter, we'll talk about HOW to choose the right strategy for you, but first, let's have a brief primer in the kinds of exit strategies that are available to you in our market, and what they can do for you.

Understanding the Exit Strategies:

From Quick Turn Cash to High Return Investments

When you first begin attending our association meetings, it might feel like everyone in the room is doing something completely different from everyone else in the room.

This guy's a wholesaler, that gal's a bird dog, this one over here is renting properties to tenants and that one over there is doing something involving collecting payments that aren't rent from people who live in his houses but aren't tenants.

In fact, you might find yourself overwhelmed by the sheer number of strategies that seem to be exercised here in the area. <u>But when you continue to come to meetings and talk to people</u>, you'll start to understand that all of these different exit strategies—no matter what the practitioners are calling them or the fine details of how they're doing them—fall into four basic categories based on the length of time that the investor is involved in them (short, medium, or long term); the intended type of income (fast cash or ongoing income); and whether or not the entrepreneur is doing any work or maintenance to the property while he owns them.

So when you choose the first exit strategy you want to pursue, you'll choose from one of these "types" of strategies.

The "Quick Turn" Strategies

There are quick-turn strategies for nearly every kind of real estate-related asset: ugly properties, pretty properties, and even mortgages and notes.

But no matter what asset is being quick-turned, ALL quick-turn strategies have these things in common:

- They involve 3 parties: the owner of the property (the seller); you; and the person who intends to own or occupy the property or asset (the end buyer)
- They give you a fast (often 20 days or less), but one-time cash payment
- Most of these strategies don't require you to "buy" the property or asset at all, but only to "tie it up" with a purchase or option agreement. Your profit comes when you sell that

agreement to a buyer, who then steps into your shoes and buys the property itself directly from the owner.

- Because you never take possession of the asset in question, you mostly don't have to have a lot of cash or credit to do them: just knowledge and skill, which is easy to get at COREE.
- You rarely make any investment in improvements to the property or asset—it's sold "as is" to the end buyer
- The profits from the transactions are taxed as ordinary income unless you take certain steps, by doing these deals through an entity like an LLC, to convert some of the income to dividends

Examples of Quick-Turn Strategies[17]

Wholesaling to Other Investors

This is probably the best-known and most-practiced quick-turn strategy in our area. Commonly called, simply, "wholesaling", this strategy involves getting properties under contract at very low prices, then selling the contracts to landlords or rehabbers at prices that allow those other investors to make a fair profit on the propert .

Typical property type: Single families, doubles, three families. Less commonly, apartment buildings, condos, mobile homes

- Typical areas: low-end rental to middle-end owner-occupied
- Typical "after repaired" values of the properties: $30,000-$150,000

---

[17] It's been a constant topic of discussion at our meetings recently that the Ohio Division of Real Estate has gone on record as saying that both wholesaling and lease/option assignments, under certain (undefined) circumstances, require a real estate license to implement. Several of the attorneys we've consulted have told us that this is not the case *as long as* the "flipper" in the transaction—you—are using appropriate contracts, advertising deals correctly, and following best practices. COREE has a members-only wholesaling focus group that meets monthly to discuss these issues (and, of course, how to make more money wholesaling). Nonetheless, you should be aware of the issue. And now you are.

- Typical condition: Extremely poor to fair
- Typical profits: $5,000-$10,00
- Typical timeframe: 5-30 days

Lease/Option Assignments (aka wholesaling lease/options, "ACTS", others)

In this strategy, it's a lease agreement with an option to buy, rather than a purchase agreement, that's assigned. The "buyer" in this case isn't really a buyer at all, but rather a homeowner wannabe who can't qualify for a conventional mortgage to purchase a home, and therefore rents (via the lease agreement) with a right to buy at a fixed price at some point in the future (via the option agreement). Your profit is made by finding sellers who are willing to accept an arrangement of this nature, negotiating a price and monthly payments, then finding buyers who can make an upfront payment (called an option fee) to you in order to step into the contract you've negotiated with the seller.

- Typical property type: Single family homes. Less commonly, condominiums.
- Typical areas: Middle end to high end owner occupied areas
- Typical "after repaired" values of the properties: $100,000-$500,000+
- Typical condition: average to excellent
- Typical profits: $5,000-$20,000, depending on the value of the property
- Typical timeframe: 5-30 days

Variations on the quick-turn strategies: wholesaling mortgages, wholesaling owner financed deals, wholesaling land, wholesaling performing or non-performing mortgages.

The Buy, Fix, Sell Strategies

One obvious way to make money with ANY asset is to purchase it, improve it, and then sell it based on its improved value.

In real estate and real estate-related assets, the "improving it" part can be physical improvement—like turning an ugly property into a pretty property through renovation—or it can involve "re-performing" the financial aspect of the real estate, as when you buy a poorly managed apartment building, kick out the bad tenants, fill up the vacancies, and sell it at an increased price based on the increased income.

The basic concept of buy/fix (or re-perform)/sell can be applied to just about any type of property or asset, including mortgages (which are "re-performed" when they're bought as defaulted loans, and a payment plan is worked out with the borrower). However, all buy/fix sell strategies involve these things:

- The properties are always purchased, not just conrolled, in order to give you full control over any renovation and/or management
- They require an investment of cash (yours, a lender's, or a partners) in purchase and, often, rehab of the property
- They are relatively short term (3 months-2 years)
- The profit in these transactions is created by increasing the value of the asset
- The lion's share—and in some cases, all—of the profit is achieved upon sale of the property or asset

Examples of Buy/Fix/Sell Strategies

Selling Fixed-Up Homes to Homeowners ("Retailing")

Thanks to the popularity of T.V. shows like *Flip This House*, even non-investors are familiar with this strategy. Conceptually, it's simple to understand: buy a house, improve it, sell it to a homeowner at a price that's higher than your purchase price + repair costs + holding and finance costs + sale costs. But the devil is, of course, in the details, and this strategy requires a LOT of attention to the details.

- Typical property type: Single family homes
- Typical areas: Middle-end homeowner areas
- Typical "after repaired" values of the properties: $90,000-$150,000
- Typical condition: At purchase, poor to fair. At resale, above average to excellent
- Typical profits: $15,000-$30,00
- Typical timeframe: 2-6 months

Selling Fixed-Up, Performing Rentals to Landlords (Selling Turnkey Rentals)

The bear market of 2008-2012 caused a resurgence in interest in "passive" real estate investments, both among individuals looking to rebuild their cratered retirement investments and amongst private equity funds (commonly called "hedge funds") that pool money from passive investors and use it to buy rental properties. Many of these individuals and companies want to be as hands-off as possible in the process of renovating, renting, and managing these properties, and are looking to acquire true "turn-key" properties.

As a result, a strategy has sprung up in affordable markets like Central Ohio that involves finding distressed, under-market properties, renovating them to rental standards, qualifying and putting in a tenant, then selling the properties, often with management in place.

- Typical property type: Single family homes. More rarely, 2-3 family properties
- Typical areas: low-end rental areas to low-end owner occupied areas

- Typical "after repaired" values of the properties: $30,000-$100,000
- Typical condition: At purchase, poor to fair. At resale, average to good.
- Typical profits: $10,000-$25,00
- Typical timeframe: 2 months-1 year

Other variations on Buy/Fix/Sell: Purchasing and repositioning apartment buildings and commercial properties; buying defaulted notes and mortgage, "re-performing" them (that is, getting the borrowers on a new payment plan that they can afford), and selling the re-performing paper

Buy to Hold Strategies

Buy to hold strategies are the only strategies in real estate that even start to approach the concept of actual "investing", which is to say that money is invested and a long-term return (hopefully a positive one) results.

The main variations in buy to hold strategies are in the type of asset you might choose to buy in the first place. Put any ten local buy-and-hold fans in a room together, and they'll argue all day long about whether houses, apartments, strip malls, self-storage facilities, mobile home parks, or any of a dozen other types of investment property are the "best"—and it's a debate worth having, since each class of property has its own pros and cons. But whatever it is you choose to buy and hold, you'll find that all the investments have certain things in common.

- You'll always purchase the asset or control it via an entity that you own
- Because you purchase the asset, there will be an investment of cash (yours, a lender's, or a partners) in purchase and, often, rehab of the property
- Unlike the properties in categories 1 and 2, which are valued

based on their immediate resale value in the market, buy and hold assets are valued based on their potential for return on investment

- They are long term. The expectation is always that the asset will begin producing returns relatively quickly, and that these returns will increase over time

- The profits are created in several ways: through income from the asset (that is, rent); through increasing equity in the property as any underlying financing is paid o f; and through increasing value of the property via appreciation and inflation

- These investments are generally tax-advantaged in multiple ways, including the allowance of depreciation write-offs, the fact that rental income is not subject to self-employment taxes, the availability of section 1031 tax-deferred exchanges to eliminate capital gains taxes, write-offs on interest expenses, and more

Partnering With/Provide Financing For Buyers

This category of exit strategy is perhaps the most complex to explain to the inexperienced investor. The basic thing that makes it profitable and in-demand is this: lots of buyers of real estate, including both owner-occupants and other investors, want properties, but don't have the money to buy them for cash or the credit to qualify for traditional loans.

Therefore, if you have a property, and you're willing to take payments rather than demanding that a buyer bring the entire purchase price to the table, you can 1) get a higher purchase price for the property and 2) charge a higher interest rate than traditional lenders do. These two things lead to very high returns for the investors who understand how to do them.

The complexity in this strategy is that these transactions take a lot of different forms, and each has different tax and legal consequences to you as what we will loosely call "the lender". But in general, these strategies do have certain things in common:

- They don't necessarily require that you "own" the property, in the sense that the deed is in your name, but they do require that you at least "control" the property via some legal contract like a lease/option or contract for deed/land contract.

- Although this is not a requirement of these strategies, from a practical perspective, most investors sell the properties "as is", without making any repairs or improvements

- In today's market, they are medium to long term strategies. At the height of the real estate lending mania in, say, 2005-2006, it was possible to offer buyers short term financing and expect them to go to a bank and get a loan of their own in 6 months-1 year. Today, with tighter lending criteria, you can expect to collect payments for 2-15 years before the buyer either secures conventional financing or pays o f the loan through natural amortization

- Uniquely among the four categories, the profit from these deals can come at 3 different points in the deal: up front, through the down payment or deposit; monthly, though a "spread" in the payments you receive vs. any payments that you make; and at the end, if there is a balloon in the loan requiring a lump sum payment from the "buyer"

Fully explaining each of these forms, their pros and cons, the properties on which they can be exercised, the state and national laws that govern them[18], and the various types of borrowers could literally take up an entire book in itself. So, instead, let's look at some common types of this strategy used here in the area.

---

[18] The most important of which is the Dodd-Frank act, which regulates any transaction in which the person making payments is an owner-occupant. COREE members can download an explanation of Dodd-Frank and what's required to comply with it and avoid serious penalties at www.CentralOhioREIA.com

"Sandwiching" Owner Financing

The immediate thought that many local investors have when they hear about the idea of buying a house and then selling it with owner financing is, "The problem is, I'm one of those people who doesn't have the cash or credit to buy a property in the first place!"

That's why one of the most common strategies in this category rely on an ENTRANCE strategy of BUYING the property with owner financing, as well. In these scenarios, you find a seller who is willing to take payments—whether by allowing you to "assume" his existing mortgage, or, if his property is paid off, by carrying a seller-held mortgage with acceptable monthly payments FROM you. You then find a buyer—typically an owner-occupant, in these cases—who is willing and able to make the upfront payment, the monthly payments, and meet any balloon you might put into the financing

A typical scenarios for this kind of deal might be: You buy a nice 3 bedroom ranch from the owner "subject to" the existing $105,000 mortgage with payments of $750/month and no money down. You then lease the property with an option to buy to a nice young couple for $125,000 with $5,000 down (your first profit check), monthly rent of $1,000 (for a $250/month profit), and a 3 year term, at which point you'll collect your remaining $15,000 in profit ($120,000 purchase price - $5,000 already collected down - $100,000 now owed to the seller's bank)

- Typical property type: Single family homes
- Typical areas: middle to high-end owner occupied areas
- Typical "after repaired" values of the properties: $100,000+
- Typical condition: Average to excellent
- Typical profits: $20,000-$50,000, spread out over the term of the deal
- Typical timeframe: 2-5 years

"Repair for Equity" Deals

There is a basic problem with selling properties that need work to be ready to live in in today's market: there's no conventional financing available for people who want to buy them, no matter how good a deal the property might be or how qualified the buyer might be to make the necessary repairs.

This has led to a roaring revival of a type of arrangement that was popular prior to the financing madness of the early part of this century: the "Repair for Equity" deal. In these scenarios, buyers (sometimes investor/renovators, sometimes homeowners) who have the will, experience, and resources to make repairs to a property buy it from you with a small down payment but at a higher price than you could sell it for if you were requiring the buyer to bring his own money to the table.

A typical scenario for this kind of deal might be: You buy a beat-up, older house in a marginal area for $15,000. You sell it to a contractor for $29,000 with $1,000 down at 8% interest, secured by a mortgage and note or a contract for deed. The resulting monthly payments are $339/month + taxes and insurance for 10 years, at which point the buyer owns the property free and clear. As the "lender", you have no expenses on the property, which makes your actual yield somewhere between 25% and infinit , depending on whether you paid cash for the property or financed it initiall .

- Typical property type: For handy homeowners: single family homes. For investor/renovators: any kind of income property
- Typical areas: Any, but usually rental to mid-level owner occupied
- Typical "after repaired" values of the properties: $30,000-?
- Typical condition: poor to fair
- Typical profits: Depends on the price range of the property being sold. Returns, if property is purchased right, are in the 20%-50% range.
- Typical timeframe: 5-15 years

The Most Important Thing You'll Do In Your Entire Real Estate Career:

How to Choose the Right Exit Strategy

Too many people fall into the trap of picking a strategy—and, often, investing in expensive education about that strategy—based on hype, or momentary excitement, or emotion, or simple lack of information that there's more than one thing that can be done in real estate. At our association, we're constantly hearing guests say things like:

"I bought some rentals because my uncle's a big-time landlord and I've seen what it's done for him, but what I really need is to pay off my $25,000 in credit card bills because the monthly payments are sucking me dry. Is there some way that real estate could help me with that?"

Or...

"I was listening to a webinar and I got super-excited about wholesaling, so I spent $5,000 on a course, but I have a really high-income job and Uncle Sam is taking 50% of my profits. What I really need is retirement income, how do I get that?"

Or, saddest of all...

"I spent $25,000 on a complete soup-to-nuts program from a national seminar company about how to do everything with every property, and now I'm practically a Ph.D. in real estate, but I can't do a deal because I'm hopelessly confused about where to start."

Mark my words: **there is one, and only one, correct way to choose an exit strategy, and it's to decide first what YOU need in your financial life**.

It doesn't matter what made your friend rich.

It doesn't matter what the guru said was the "only" way or "hottest" way or "best" way to make money in real estate today.

It doesn't even matter what your fellow COREE members are doing, or are telling you that you should do—unless, of course, they know your particular situation, in which case you might want to consider their experienced advice.

Whatever you need—quick cash, long-term income, tax breaks, growth—there's an exit strategy that you can implement right here in your own back yard that will provide it. So the proper order in which to make the very-important decision about exit strategy is this:

1. **Sit down—with your significant other, if you have one— and take a look at your financial situation.** What do you MOST need to correct or improve that situation right now? Is it to pay off consumer debt? Build reserves? Set up income for retirement? Start saving for the kids' college education? Put aside money for health care?

2. **Learn about the basic exit strategies from a high-level view.** What are they? What do they require in the way of time, money, credit, and other resources? What kind of money to they generate, and how much money, and how often?

3. **Choose 1 or 2 exit strategies that best meet your goals, and invest in studying them in depth**. Once you've narrowed down the options, it makes sense to invest some time and money in learning the

In-depth workshops, bootcamps, and home study courses can be expensive, and vary enormously in quality. One great use of your COREE membership is to get advice from other members about the quality of any course BEFORE you buy. Trust me, the "today only" deal will still be available after you've gotten some objective opinions on the content!

exact tactics, methods, documents, and practices needed to implement your chosen strategy. <u>Any successful practitioner of real estate, in any strategy, will tell you that this is how THEY learned what to do (and just as importantly, what NOT to do), and that buying an expert's system is generally MUCH cheaper (and quicker to implement) than making all the rookie mistakes yourself.</u>

4. **Implement your exit strategy and continue to learn, making adjustments as necessary**. Do what needs to be done, over and over, even when it's scary and frustrating, until it works. When you have questions or run into problems, don't give up—ask your fellow association members how to overcome them and move on. Above all, don't get distracted by other "opportunities"—if you did what you were supposed to and chose your strategy for a thought-out, logical reason, just because the next speaker at the next association meeting is doing something completely different doesn't mean that you should, too.

5. **Reach your goal, set a new one**. Once you've taken care of your immediate cash needs, or built the reserves, or put aside enough money or assets to pay for college, you might well find that it s time to explore a new strategy—maybe one that builds more passive income for retirement. Or perhaps you're on track for a prosperous retirement, and the next goal is to create enough current income to quit your job. In any case, it's fine to learn the next exit strateg , and the next, and the next— but only AFTER you've implemented the first

LESSON 2

Never Pay Retail. Not Ever. Ever. (and how to find under-market deals)

There's an old saying among experienced real estate investors that goes, "You make your money when you BUY." And while I'm not a big believer in conventional wisdom for conventional wisdom's sake, you'll find that this particular old saw is pretty much dead-on accurate.

"You make your money when you buy" is a shorthand way of saying "If you get a good deal at the start of the deal, it's pretty easy to make money. If you make a bad deal at the beginning, it's pretty hard to make money."

And for us, as real estate entrepreneurs, getting a good deal means one or both of these things:

1. Buying at a price that is significantly—like 30% or more below the current, as-is value of the property AND/OR

2. Buying on terms that are significantly better than "market terms"—low or no down payment, low or no interest rate, small or even no monthly payments, no qualifying based on credit or income, and so on.

In other words, We. Don't. Pay. Retail.

Ever.

In some of the strategies we discussed in the last chapter, it's

31

obvious WHY you can't pay full price, or even close to full price, for a property. If your intention is to repair and sell the property quickly, or to wholesale it to another investor immediately, your profit is <u>only</u> guaranteed if you pay an under-market price.

But even if your plan is to buy rental properties, paying full price and getting conventional financing generally doesn't work as a money-making strategy. One or the other, maybe, but not both. Unfortunately, the reasons for this become clear only AFTER you've made the purchase, so let me save you some pain and fill you in on the secret of why you don't want to make this rookie mistake:

Cash flow $\neq$ Rent – (principal + interest + taxes + insurance

There are other, significant expenses involved in owning rental properties. Vacancy losses, turnover costs, and maintenance alone will cost you 20-30% of your gross rents on a single family home. "Reserves"—the money you put aside for that moment in 20 years when the brand-new roof (and furnace, and windows, and water heater, and driveway, and and and) needs to be replaced—are another 10% that you shouldn't consider profits.

Take any rental you own or have considered purchasing and do this formula:

Rent

-30% of gross rent (for vacancy, maintenance, and reserves)

-taxes and insurance

<u>-your monthly mortgage payment, if you pay full price, put 20% down, and finance conventionall</u> [19]

Your net monthly cash flo

---

[19]   If you're not sure how to calculate this number, just Google "free mortgage calculator" and enter the interest rate, loan amount, and term of the loan

Is that number under that line really enough to excite you? Like, enough to own and maintain that house and deal with those tenants and all their problems?

Now do this one:

(Your net monthly cash flow x 12) ÷ Your upfront cash investment in down payment, loan costs, and initial repairs

Multiply the number you get by 100, and that's your rate of return on the cash you invested. Excited now? Because if that number is less than 12%, you could have done better by investing in someone else's deal, passively.

So how, you might ask, does not paying retail "fix" the low cash flow and low rate of return problem? Easy: by lowering the loan amount (borrowing 80% of 100% of the value means a bigger loan than borrowing 80% of 70% of the value), or by lowering the monthly payment by getting a lower interest rate on the loan.

And we're just getting started on all the great reasons that you shouldn't pay retail for properties. . Here are a few more:

Buying under market means that you can liquidate quickly, without taking a bath. Each and every week, I talk to landlords who desperately want to sell one or more of their rentals. Sometimes the reasons are personal (job transfer, can't handle the tenants, divorce, increase in hours spent at work), and sometimes they're financial (property is losing money, lost job, facing foreclosure). In any case, they need to sell fast, and...

When these landlords have purchased their properties at retail in the last 2-3 years, and did what I just told you NOT to do, they usually end up walking away from all or part of the cash they invested in the property, AND sometimes bringing money to closing to pay off their loan, as well.

See, the problem is that the rental that they bought 2 years ago for $90,000 is now worth about…$85,000, because then they bought it, it had brand new carpet, was freshly painted, and had new appliances. Now it's got 5 years of tenant damage. Sure, if the owner could invest the money to bring it back into its original condition, it would be worth $92,000, but if he had that kind of time, he wouldn't be a motivated seller.

And because his loan has barely amortized, he owes $70,000 on the original $72,000 balance. Oh, and because I'm a SMART investor, I still want to pay him 70% of the $85,000 value, or $59,500. But even if he could find someone who wanted to pay 90%, he'd only STILL have to bring a few thousand dollars to the closing, because by the time he's paid his Realtor a 6% commission and paid his part of the closing costs and the transfer fees and the deed prep and so on, he'd be unlikely to net more than about $68,000 on the sale, from which he needs to pay off a $70,000 mortgage.

On the other hand, the seller who got a 30% discount when HE bought can generally sell and come close to breaking even, even if he has to sell soon after the purchase. Everyone plans to keep their rentals forever, but sometimes life gets in the way. If the worst happens, would you rather take a loss, or make a profit when you sell

Buying under market bullet-proofs your investment, whatever happens in the economy. One of the fears in the minds of many real estate investors today is that prices will take another 2008-like tumble. The idea that, except in the typical bubble markets on the east and west coasts, real estate slowly and steadily increases in value year in and year out was beaten out of all of us by the crash. Although the underlying factors that drove that historic cratering of the market aren't with us anymore, the ghost of losses past still, reasonably, haunts us.

But think of it this way: if you've purchased your property at a below-market price to begin with, a 30% drop in property values will simply bring the value of other properties in line with what you paid to begin with. You'll lose net worth on paper, but you won't lose money even if you sell. Or if you do, it will be significantl less than those around you who paid full retail for their units.

Perhaps more importantly, by buying under market, you'll have more flexibil ty to ride out economically troubled times than other, less savvy investors. Imagine that America enters another depression, with 30% of all adults out of work. Will people still need a place to live? You bet. Will they be able to pay as much rent as before? Probably not. But if you bought the property under market, and thus have a lower payment on any loan against the property, you'll theoretically be able to afford to lower your payments, thus attracting tenants even when no one else can.

All things being equal, buying under market will make you richer, quicker. Let's say you have $300,000 to invest, and you can either buy 2 rental houses that rent for $1200 each at their full values of $150,000 each, or you can buy 3 identical houses at $100,000 each. Which is better?

Well, duh. Buying 3 is better in every conceivable way. When you buy 2, you have $300,000 worth of houses that you paid $300,000 for—and thus no equity. When you buy 3, you have $450,000 worth of houses (3 at $150,000 value each) that you paid $300,000 for, and you've ADDED $150,000 to your net worth.

When you buy 2, you get $2,400 a month in gross rents for your $300,000 investment. When you buy 3, you get $3,600 a month in gross rents—for the same $300,000 investment.

Maybe you DON'T have $150,000 to start with—most of our members don't. But the same idea applies—buying cheaper means more equity, more return, and more wealth, faster.

OK, I Get It...

But Who's Gonna Let Me Buy Their Property

For Pennies on the Dollar?

I've seen hundreds of budding investors struggle with the very basic question of, "How am I ever going to find anyone who wants to sell me a house at below retail price? Why would anyone do that, when they could just find someone else to pay them more? [20]

One of the key things a real estate entrepreneur in ANY market has to learn and really, really internalize is that the real estate market is an inefficient market, and as a result, good deals can be had by those who know where to look and how to make offers.

Let me explain further, and bear with me, because understanding why there are great deals requires understanding conventional real estate sales just don't work for every seller:

A house (or apartment building or strip mall or what have you) is a big, expensive investment.

In fact, for most Americans who own real estate, it's the biggest single investment they'll ever make, and a significant percentage of their net worth will be tied up in it.

Real estate is also a relatively illiquid asset, meaning that it's hard to sell it quickly. Because most properties cost more than most people can simply pay cash for, the "conventional" method of buying properties involves putting some money down and borrowing the rest from a bank. And involving a bank—or any other traditional lender—

---

[20] And the answer is NOT "I have to find someone who doesn t know what their property is worth, and take advantage of that fact." EVERYONE today knows what their property is worth, and if they don't, they know how to go on the internet and find out. Sellers don t sell at below-retail prices and terms because they're stupid, or ignorant. They sell at below-retail prices and terms because they're MOTIVATED.

means that the property and the borrower have to meet certain criteria in order for the lender to agree to become involved in the deal.

The very process of finding out if the property and the buyer meet those criteria—an appraisal, inspection, credit check, employment verification, underwriting, and so on—takes weeks if not months...and the outcome is never certain. The property might fail; the borrower might fail; and if so, the seller is back to square one in trying to sell his property.

What's more, the conventioal way in which real estate is marketed and by which the price is negotiated is slow. Think about how stocks are sold: if you're interested in buying shares in a particular company, you're simply be able to go online (or, heck, turn on the T.V. and watch the ticker at the bottom of any of the various financial channels), find out what that stock is selling for today (in other words, how a very large number of potential buyers are valuing it right now), decide if you value it the same way, and, if so, log into your online brokerage account and place an order to buy it. 10 minutes later, you're the proud owner of those stocks.

But there aren't tens of thousands of potential buyers for any given parcel of real estate. Each of the handful of buyers who might be interested in a particular property will value it slightly differently—this one loves the fenced yard and wants to pay a little more for it, that one loves the house but doesn't like the street so much, and so will buy it, but only if he can get a discount.

And in order for a buyer and a seller of a particular property to even FIND one another, the seller has to take extraordinary steps (hiring an agent, placing and maintaining ads, and so on) to let potential buyers know that the property is for sale.

So in order for the seller of any property to turn it into money, he's typically going to:

1. Prepare the property for sale (clean it, paint it, repair it, etc), a process that can take weeks or months
2. Find a real estate agent and fill out reams of paperwork and disclosures
3. Let the real estate agent place it in MLS
4. Wait for various buyers to find the listing, make an appointment, see the property, evaluate it, and make an offer
5. Negotiate the terms of the offer
6. Wait for the buyer and the property to be approved for financing, and assuming that all goes well
7. Wait for the closing to be scheduled and occur

This is why, even in relatively 'hot' markets, it takes 60 days, on average, to sell and close on even a desirable, well-priced property. And exposing the property to the market in this way is the BEST way to get the highest possible price for any given piece of real estate.

But not every seller has that option. What if, for instance:

- The property itself has no chance of qualifying for an institutional loan, and the seller doesn't have the time or money to improve the condition to the point where a conventional lender will consider making a loan on it
- The seller is under some external time constraint that means that he can't risk waiting 60, or 90, or 300 days for the property to sell, such as an impending tax foreclosure or the need to cash out of the property quickly in order to take advantage of some other opportunity
- The seller is simply emotionally unprepared to continue to own the property—he's fed up with it, and just wants it gone

In other words, some sellers need to sell FAST a whole lot more than they need to sell for top price and all cash.

It's by finding these sellers that any successful real estate entrepreneurs buy properties of all sorts for pennies on the dollar, or with terms that you can hardly believe until you've done it yourself.

In every market, 'hot' and 'cold', there are sellers in these situations. Typical things that would tend to motivate the owner of a piece of property to sell it under the prices and terms you want include:

- The seller inherited the house, and just wants to cash out fast without doing an repairs or upgrades

- The seller is facing foreclosure for non-payment of his mortgage, or of his taxes

- The seller has had health problems that have made it impossible for him to maintain the property

One of the many advantages of belonging to Central Ohio Real Estate Entrepreneurs is the education you get about how to find and market to these sellers. Another is "Best and Worst Deals" contests, in which your fellow members share how local deals came together from finding them to negotiating them to cashing in on them.

- The seller bought the property with the intention of repairing and selling it, but ran out of money or found the renovation process too difficult. It s not finished, and he wants to be rid of it

- The seller is getting divorced, or is part of a failed partnership, and the property has to be liquidated for him to be rid of his ex-spouse or ex-partner

- The seller has had one or more bad tenants who've abused his property and not paid him, and he's sick of the whole thing

- The seller bought a new house before he sold his old one, and is now making 2 payments that he can't afford

- The seller needs to sell his old house in order to buy his new one

- The seller has moved out of the area and no longer needs the house
- The seller bought the property far from where he lives, and has found management to be too difficul
- The seller has a business opportunity that he needs money to take advantage of, and needs to sell the house to get the cash
- The city is on the seller's back about the condition of the property
- The property suffered a fire, flood, or other damage; th insurance company paid the seller for the property; the seller took the money and didn't make the repairs
- The seller is elderly and going into a nursing home and must sell the property in order to meet Medicaid requirements
- The seller won the lottery and bought a mansion and really doesn't care about his old bread-and-butter house anymore21
- The seller is a company or institution that acquired the property through foreclosure, inheritance, etc and isn't in the business of owning properties
- And dozens of other situations.

If you've ever BEEN the motivated seller of a property, for one of these or any other reason, you know how grateful you were when a ready, willing, and able buyer showed up with a solution—even when that solution was not a full-price cash offer.

If you want to buy properties cheap, all you have to do is be the person with that solution, and find the seller who needs it. And when you learn to do that, you never need to pay retail price or terms for a property.

---

[21] Yes, that actually happened to me once. I got a fully fixed up $90,000 for $25,000 because the guy who owned it won the lottery the previous week and couldn't wait to get into the new mansion he'd already bought.

LESSON 3

Forget About Being a "Self Made" Millionaire

Don't get me wrong: there are tens of thousands--maybe hundreds of thousands--of people in the United States right now with 7 and 8 figure net worths who got it ALL because they started and grew a real estate investing business.

And most of these folks will tell you that when they started, they had little or no spare cash, and no special real estate acumen, and not much in the way of a credit score.

So, yes, in the sense that you can be born without a silver spoon in your mouth, and live a pretty average life, and even make some big giant financial mistakes along the way, and still end up in the top 10% of all Americans in terms of your assets and income, it's possible to be a "self-made" real estate mogul.

But when you look closely at the really successful real estate entrepreneurs around you, you'll notice something that they all have in common: a team of experts they've built over the years to do the things that have to be done to run a real estate business, but that aren't actually part of the "money making" process. And from this perspective, they aren't self-made at all, but rather "team-made".

The Two Kinds of Activities in Your

Real Estate Business

There are 2 kinds of tasks you'll find yourself faced with in starting--and particularly in growing--your real estate business. First, there are the ones the directly make you money, including:

- Talking to motivated sellers
- Making decisions about what to pay for a property, and on what terms
- Making decisions about and managing renovations to a property
- Making decisions about how to price a property for rental or sale
- Choosing appropriate tenants
- Negotiating with buyers and renters

Second, and it's a much longer list, there are the task that are necessary to 'keep the trains running on time', as it were, but which actually distract you from doing the things that add to your bottom line. These include:

- Mailing out marketing, hanging bandit signs,[22] putting ads in craigslist
- Balancing the bank accounts
- Preparing and filing taxe
- Doing title work on a property you're proposing to buy
- Mowing lawns, cleaning hallways, and other routine maintenance

---

[22]   If you're not familiar with this particular piece of jargon, it refers to those plastic signs that say something like "I Buy Houses" and hang on telephone poles in a neighborhood near you. Yes, they're against code and, in some people's opinion, a serious eyesore, but they are also very effective.

- Showing vacant units [23]
- Creating and maintaining your website
- Maintaining and updating your computers, software, and equipment
- Coordinating and performing closings to buy, sell, and rent properties
- Inspecting houses for termites and other wood destroying pests
- Taking maintenance calls from tenants that will just be referred to the maintenance guy anyway

- And there are literally 100 others I could list.

You'll note that some of these things are simply rote work that a low-paid administrator or maintenance person can easily do, while some are things that professionals like accountants, title companies, attorneys, and coders can actually do better, more easily, and more professionally than you can.

Yes, you will meet real estate entrepreneurs who take pride in the fact that they do literally everything it takes to keep their business up and running, from book keeping and tax preparation to doing their own title searches and closings to performing their own work on their properties.

But the really successful ones--the ones that you most want to be like--understand that the sheer amount of time and energy it takes to learn and execute all of these activities limits the amount of wealth and income they can build, not to mention the time they have to

---

[23] Every long-time landlord reading this is thinking, "what do you mean this doesn't make me money? Vacancies are expensive! Filling them is a money-making priority!" Agreed--but the question I'd have for you is, "Is waiting on a front porch for a prospect that you know perfectly well only has a 60% chance of showing up at all, and a 20% chance of showing up AND applying, and a 10% chance of showing up, applying, and passing the application process a good use of your time?" 'Cause if you have a better use for those hours, there's this thing called a lockbox...

The very best way to quickly build a team of reliable, affordable, investor-friendly service providers is to ask your colleagues at COREE who they use to perform various roles in their businesses. This benefit of membership will save you enormous time, keep you from making expensive mistakes by hiring the wrong people, and generally make your rise to riches a whole lot faster and easier!

enjoy it. Whenever there are professionals out there who can do any job as well as or better than you can, it's almost always to your advantage to pay them to do it, and use your own time more profitabl .

A common example of this is renovators who, rather than supervising the work on their properties, actually do some or all of it themselves.

Often, these are folks who come from a building or contracting background, and figure that the fastest, surest, and cheapest way to get repairs done is to do it themselves. But the flaw in this seemingly-logical thought is that, in terms of potential dollars per hour worked, renovation does not pay nearly as well as deal-hunting.

Look at it like this: if you're a skilled painter, you might be able to paint a 1200 square foot home in less than three 8-hour days. And hiring another skilled painter to do the job might cost you $1500 in labor. If you do the work yourself, you've saved–and therefore, have effectively been PAID–$1500 for 3 days' work.

If you're used to trading your hours for dollars like that, you might just think that saving $1,500 is a pretty good way to spend 3 days. But when you understand how to find, negotiate, finance, and sell real estate, spending those 3 days painting at $500 a day is an unforgivable waste of your time.

Why? Because if you'd just hired a painter to do the work and spent that half a week finding another deal, and, let's say, wholesaling it for a mere $5,000 cash profit, you'd clearly be able to pay the painter AND,

I don't know, go to Mexico for a week.

And the same applies to many functions that you COULD perform in your own business, but probably shouldn't. And that's where your "team" comes in.

Your team is a group of experts and professionals who you pay for labor, services, and advice as needed. Your team members are not necessarily employees–in fact, most will be independent contractor who serve other real estate entrepreneurs, as well. But, like employees, they need to be people who are great at what they do, whom you trust and get along with, and who ultimately add to your bottom line.

You will build your team over time, as you meet and network with the people who provide the products and services you need. You will add team members as needed, replace them where necessary, and–above all–make the relationship profitable and easy for THEM as well as for yourself.

Your Team Members

The team you need depends in part on how much investing you are doing, and, even more so, on which strategies you're employing. For instance, wholesalers don't typically need maintenance companies or property managers; people who fix and resell houses don't need eviction attorneys.

So, ultimately, you'll pick and choose from this list to build the team that will help you become a team-made millionaire.

Your Real Estate Agent. Most successful real estate investors have a real estate agent on their team, and the reason is more complex than you might think.

A good real estate agent can do a lot more than help you find, look at, and make offers on properties that are listed through the Multiple

Listing Service. A GOOD agent--one who understands real estate as an investment, not just as a product to be sold for a commission--can also help you choose the right areas in which to buy properties for rental or resale by researching things like average time on the market for resale, sale prices of similar properties, and so on.

Your agent can also take some of the chores related to closing properties off your back. For instance, he can work with your lender in scheduling appraisals and inspections, provide your closing agent with a legal description and loan payoff, and work with the seller or his agent to overcome any problems during the process.

A really good agent will also aggressively negotiate on your behalf, acting in your best interest to get the price and terms you want for each property.

And when you're first getting started, your agent will also be able to explain some of the technicalities of the offer process, including how much earnest money is typically offered in your area, how to fill out the purchase contract, how long to leave the offer open, and so on. And, of course, your agent can also list and market a finished property, if you decide to fix and resell it

Unfortunately, real estate agents who are both pro-investor and relatively knowledgeable about investment strategies are few and far between. Most agents are formally trained to do one thing and one thing only: sell properties to qualified home owners, who want homes in good condition, who pay retail prices, and who get their financing from traditional lenders. It is often difficult or impossible for you to overcome this training and convince a particular agent that you really do want to see ugly, smelly houses that you can buy for pennies on the dollar. It's the rare agent who recognizes that it's better to have a client who buys 10 houses a year, year in and year out, at $50,000 each than to have one client who buys a $200,000 home once every 5 years.

So in choosing your agent, you need one who is:

- Comfortable with presenting and defending lower-than-asking price offers
- Willing to accept the fact that 19 out of 20 of your offers will be rejected–sometimes angrily
- Willing to keep you updated on a weekly basis on new properties on the market that fit your criteri
- Knowledgeable about–or willing to learn–the ins and outs of your strategy
- Willing to research additional information about neighborhoods, property values, and so on
- Not competing with you for the same properties–that is, not investing in the same houses and areas that you are

Often, this agent is a relatively new licensee who has few listings and a limited client base. These are the folk who are most likely to have the time and energy to do what you need them to do–and are the most open to learning how to be an investor's agent.

And, by the way, **you do not typically pay your buyer's agent for his services**–the seller does. But when you find a great agent who makes you a lot of money, don't hesitate to "tip" him by sending a little extra cash to his broker, or taking him out to a nice dinner, or making some other gesture of appreciation. Remember, you want to stay at the TOP of his list when a great deal comes across his desk!

A home inspector. One of the key skills you'll need to acquire in your pursuit of real estate riches will be the ability to quickly determine what a property needs in order to be rented or resold. Most successful real estate entrepreneurs spend no more than 30 minutes in a single family home examining the condition of the systems and cosmetics before they write an offer to the seller based on what they've seen.

But those offers almost always contain an "inspection contingency" allowing you to hire a professional (or get a friend in the business) to go over the property with a fine-toothed comb before you actually have to purchase it.

This process--which is only instigated once you've already agreed on a price with the seller--is usually completed by a professional home inspector.

A home inspector's job is to spend several hours carefully examining the systems and structure of properties looking for defects that could come back to haunt you later. A good home inspector has a detailed system and special equipment for accomplishing this job, and can do it a whole lot better than you can.

Your ideal home inspector will have at least 5 year's experience, plus a background in engineering or construction. I prefer inspectors who are certified by the American Society of Home Inspectors (ASHI), as ASHI inspectors are required to achieve a certain level of education and experience before becoming certified

A home inspection costs $250-$450 for a single family home. Properties with more units will cost more to inspect. But this is a small price to pay to uncover problems that could potentially cost you thousands if they go undiscovered.

Again, you will schedule a home inspection only after you have an accepted offer, with a contingency that the inspection must meet with your approval. And always accompany your home inspector when he inspects your potential purchase–I promise, you'll get a great seminar in how properties are built and how they deteriorate.

A pest inspector. Why, you might ask, do you need both a pest inspector AND a property inspector? Because wood-destroying pests are surprisingly common in this part of the country, and critters like termites, carpenter ants, powder-post beetles, dry rot, and other wood-destroying organisms that create expensive structural damage. Because home inspectors don't look for the most pernicious little pests in the country today--bedbugs. And because pest inspections are MUCH cheaper than whole-house inspections, generally costing less than $100, and so are a kind of no-brainer when you're acquiring a property to rehab and sell or to keep.

Unlike whole-house inspections, pest inspections are typically done by the same companies that treat[24] the problem, so watch for inspectors who find pests every time they look--unfortunately, some inspectors commonly find phantom termites that need to be treated with real, $1,200 pesticides. Still, it's better to know that there's a problem and negotiate with the seller about who's going to pay for it BEFORE you close, than to find that problem after you're already the owne .

A title agent or closing attorney. In Ohio, the work needed to get to a closing (the title search, deed preparation, tax prorations, and preparation of the closing statement) are traditionally held at a title company rather than an attorney's office, as is the case in some other parts of the country.

Your closing agent is one of the most important people on your team, so it's crucial to chose one who understands that many of your transactions will not be "typical" closings with a buyer, a seller, and a conventional lender.

For instance, if you plan to wholesale properties, your title agent needs to understand how an assignment of contract works.

If your financing is coming from the seller or a private lender, he must be able to prepare and file the right documents to protect the lender's interest in the property.

---

[24] By which I mean kill, of course. "Treating" sounds like they're getting chiropractic help or something. Which would be sort of silly, since they're invertebrates.

If you are buying rentals, he needs to understand how to prorate the rents to the day of closing, and how to account for the deposits, which should be turned over to you at the closing.

In other words, your closing agent should be someone who has experience working with investors and the deals they do.

A handyperson and/or a general contractor and/or subcontractors. If you choose a strategy that requires renovation and/or ongoing maintenance of properties, one of the most important components of your team will be reliable, competent, affordable folks who can do this sort of work.

Unfortunately, reliable, competent, affordable contractors are amongst the most difficult members of your team to find and keep. Just about any investor/renovator can tell you endless stories about contractors who covered up, rather than repairing, major problems in a property; who left a job half done and disappeared from the face of the earth; who didn't bother to pull needed permits, or didn't pay his subcontractors and caused a lien to be placed against your property, or forged a worker's comp certificate, then got hurt on the job, and sued the owner for his injuries.

> COREE keeps a list of member-recommended contractors on its website at CentralOhioREIA.com. As a COREE member, you have access to this list as a resource, and you can also contribute your favorite contractors and suppliers to it.

The very best way to find people for this part of your team is simply to network with Association members. Asking your colleagues who they've used for roof work, window replacement, floor refinishing, clean up, yard work, and so on will generally yield a plethora of recommendations, both pro and con. While the fact that Joe Contractor did a great job for your fellow rehabber doesn't guarantee he'll do the same for you, it's a pretty good sign that he'll work out.

A bookkeeper and/or accountant. You'll need a bookkeeper when you own so many properties that keeping track of the incoming and outgoing payments begins to take up a significant portion of your time. You'll need an accountant almost as soon as you begin buying investment properties.

As a real estate investor (or the owner of any small business, for that matter), you'll quickly discover that your largest expense is income taxes.

Furthermore, you'll find yourself bogged down in a morass of new tax forms for calculating and reporting rental income, capital gains, depreciation, self-employment and alternative minimum taxes, and literally dozens of other brand-new requirements foisted upon you by the various taxing authorities.

Filling out this paperwork yourself is a major waste of your time, and a good, competent account WHO UNDERSTANDS REAL ESTATE can show you dozens of little-known, legal ways to save and defer taxes.

The key to that sentence is, of course, "Accountant who understands real estate". Most, frankly, don't, and few will admit that their grasp on your available deductions is less-than-adequate. [25]

Again, the best way to find a good accountant is to find out which one other investors in your area are using. No matter how married you are to the guy who's been doing your taxes since you were in college, you'll want to switch to one of the handful of tax people who do most of the tax work for most of the investors and landlords in any given area. The difference will be thousands of dollars a year in your pocket.

---

[25] Want to check whether yours does? Ask him what dealer status is, and why it will cost you an extra 12% in taxes on your wholesale and retail deals. Ask him what the tax treatment of a property sold on land contract is. Ask him whether you'll be subject to passive loss limitations on your rentals. If he says something along the lines of, "Duh, huh?" you have the wrong accountant.

An insurance agent. You'd think finding an insurance agent for your rentals and rehabs would be as easy as falling off a log. Surely that talking lizard has a product for you, right? Or maybe Flo?

But it's a little more complicated than that. Amazingly. most insurance agents don't have products for, or don't understand how to, appropriately insure non owner occupied properties. And since you may not know, either, finding the right agent is pretty important.

At a minimum, you should have a policy on each property to protect against loss and liability; a business insurance policy that covers your equipment, computers, and staff; and an umbrella liability policy of $1-$2 million (that's right, MILLION dollars) to cover you for the things the other policies don't. A good agent will also talk to you about your needs for key person insurance, disability, and other insurance you may want or need as a business owner.

The right insurance agent for you will also know how to properly write policies to insure properties owned by partnerships, corporations, limited liability companies, trusts, and other entities you might form. He'll understand what type of insurance to write when you've bought a property via an option or contract for deed, and are not the titleholder. He'll know how to name your private lenders on the policy so that their financial interests are protected

Yes, any old agent can sell you a policy. Your agent needs to have at least a basic understanding of what you do to insure you properly.

A real estate attorney. As a real estate entrepreneur, you'll need legal advice from time to time. From document preparation to reliable information about tenant/landlord law, contract law, fair housing, agency, and related issues.

And if you're smart, this person is NOT going to be the lawyer who handled your divorce, or drafted your will, or settled your car accident case.

One of the most important benefits of COREE membership is access to Ohio-specific forms and contracts through our participation in OREIA. Check out www.CentralOhioREIA.com for more information.

Most attorneys are generalists, meaning that they'll take any case that comes along. Avoid these folks at all costs, and look for a specialist who's had additional training and experience in the field of real estate. Otherwise, the advice you get will be of limited value to you–and indeed, could get you into trouble.

A corporate attorney. In a later lesson, we'll talk about the importance of good business set up both for asset protection and tax-minimizing purposes.

Once you're convinced that you need an LLC, and you will be, the next step is to make sure that the lawyer you're hiring to set it up for you understands what he's doing. Just as you need an attorney who specializes in real estate to handle your real estate transactions, you need one who specializes in asset protection to draft and file your limited partnerships, corporations, trusts, and LLCs.

A private lender, partner, or other form of "money person"[26]. We'll discuss more about the "why" of using Other People's Money (OPM) in the later chapter on creative finance. But one of the "hows" is by finding one or more people with some unused cash who'd like to invest it in real estate, passively.

Private lenders and partners are individuals who take advantage of the safety and relatively high returns of real estate WITHOUT the management, rehab, and liability problems that accompany ownership. They do this by providing mortgage loans to investors (if they're private

---

[26] It's important to note that partnering with or borrowing money from others is an activity heavily regulated by the state and federal government. We strongly recommend that you understand the rules around advertising, disclosure, registration, and so on before pursuing private money.

lenders) under terms agreed to between the investor and lender, or by providing money in return for partial ownership (if they're partners).

Unfortunately, unlike many of the other service providers you'll have on your team, money people can't be found simply by Googling them or even asking your fellow association members. Yes, you'll find non-traditional lenders--commonly called hard money lenders--that will make short term, high-rate loans without most of the qualifications of conventional loan openly advertising their services at COREE.

But the kind of longer-term financing you need to buy and hold properties comes primarily from individuals who DON'T advertise that they're interested in such investments. In fact, many don't even know that being a lender for or partner in real estate is an option, until you tell them so.

This is why you don't so much "find" private lenders and partners, as DEVELOP them. You determine, based on your exit strategy, what you'll offer in the way of interest or profits. You find people who have money. You explain why your deal or business is a good investment. You disclose the risks. You have the paperwork drawn up. YOU drive the entire transaction and relationship.

Private money people will be a crucial part of your team, especially as your business grows and more and more deals start coming your way. The entire area--how to set up deals, find potential lenders, do the paperwork, and so on--deserves your attention and study.

But for now, suffice it to say that potential lenders are all around you. Your family, friends, colleagues, and acquaintances are all waiting to hear about this great investment opportunity–even if they don't know it yet. When you realize that institutional lenders can no longer serve your needs for speed and flexibilit , start putting the word out that you're looking for private funds, and you'll be surprised at the response you get.

A mentor or coach. Most real estate entrepreneurs find that their paths to success are much straighter and less littered with obstacles when they have an experienced mentor or coach to assist them in their journey.

In fact, most wealthy local investors can trace their success back through a series of mentors and coaches who served various roles at various points in their careers. A good advisor's ability to motivate you, cut through the fear and uncertainty about investing in real estate, and even analyze and make recommendations about specific deals makes your mentor or coach potentially the most important person on your success team.

A mentor is someone whom you can turn to for guidance and motivation. Your mentor should be someone who is already where you want to be. He should be willing to share information freely. He should have ethical standards in conducting his business that match your own.

At the same time, one of the most important aspects of the mentor/ student relationship is reasonable expectations and demands on the part of the mentee. Yes, there are experienced investors out there who will simply take a shine to you, and out of the goodness of their own hearts and a desire to "give back" to the industry will go to extraordinary lengths to help you succeed, with no thought of compensation whatsoever.

But there are a lot more experienced folks who don't have the time to have lunch with you every week, hold your hand when you're scared, let you "work for free, for the experience", or otherwise turn you into a successful competitor just for the good karma.

But you'll find that, especially within the boundaries of monthly association meetings, many of your more experienced colleagues are very willing to answer questions about neighborhoods, deals, strategies, service providers, gurus, and more. Don't be afraid to ask these questions; many advanced investors get a bit of a thrill by passing on hard-earned knowledge and experience to someone who soaks it up like a sponge, then uses it to better their own lives.

On the other hand, be warned that not everyone who might want to "help" you has your best interests at heart. Sadly, there's a breed of bad guy out there that prey on newbies by offering "assistance" that's really meant to separate you from your money.

Beware of the "mentor" who actively courts you, promising to show you exactly how they buy, renovate, and manage properties. Yes, they'll put you in their car and take you out to see all the great deals they've done.

And then they'll show you a property that they happen to want to sell, and describe in glowing terms what a great deal it is, and then realize that hey, IT'S THE PERFECT FIRST DEAL FOR YOU!!! Since the property fits everything you know about what makes a great deal–knowledge that has been imparted to you by this very seller–you go for it. It's only later that you realize that the property is worth less than you thought and needs more work. But by then, your "mentor" has moved on to the next fresh fish

The easiest and most inexpensive way to get legitimate, objective advice on your deals is to join COREE's Express Success program. It includes unlimited email coaching, and costs less than $800 annually. Learn more at www.CentralOhioREIA.com

One of the most obvious warning signs of this particular species of shark is that they will make every effort to separate you from the objective advice and multiple opinions you can get from your association.

They'll invite you to special, non-club-related, "VIP only" meetings. They'll tell you that the group is full of losers and wanna-bes, and that you're wasting your time by attending meetings. They'll do anything they can to separate you from the herd, because chances are, the herd knows exactly who they are and what they're about, and will tell you not to work with them.

Find and take advantage of the knowledge of as many experienced, ethical, active coaches and mentors as you can find. But be careful that you're taking the right advice from the right people, and that you're always in a position to get multiple opinions on what you're doing.

This is a very basic list of the team members that most real estate entrepreneurs need; there will certainly be others that you add as your real estate business progresses. For instance, many real estate investors have a personal assistant to take care of the miscellaneous things you need done to keep your personal and business life in order. You may decide that you need a web designer or database designer when you begin to use the web to market to buyers, sellers, and renters, and so on. If you decide to make real estate your full time business, you'll undoubtedly end up hiring virtual or on-site receptionists, assistants, and more.

How to Make Your Team Relationships Work

As you put together your team, remember that your relationship with each team member should be win-win. For many of your team members, the "win" in working with you is that you bring repeat business to them.

But it's just as important that you remain loyal to them, treat them with respect, and, of course, pay them on time and in full.

Part of the "win" for you is having professionals in different areas that can relieve you of some of the day-to-day drudgery of owning and managing properties, but don't hesitate to add to your side of the equation by asking your service providers for discounts based on the amount of business you do with them. Most are happy to provide these discounts in return for the ease of doing business with the same person over and over: for instance, I pay $250 for closings at a company that normally charges $400–but I'm also one of the company's best customers.

A last tip on developing your success team: when you find someone who makes you a lot of money or saves you a lot of hassle, be sure to go the extra mile in making sure they know they're appreciated. The occasional thank you note is always appropriate, but for bigger wins (the real estate agent who negotiates the deal that you wholesale for a $10,000 profit, or the attorney who comes in on Christmas eve to file the LLC you need before New Year's Day, or the title company that saves the closing that ultimately makes you $25,000), make sure you express your thanks in gifts and cash.

Lesson 4

Understanding Creative Finance Lets You Buy All the Properties You Could Ever Want

How many properties would you like to buy this year? 1? 5? 25? 125?

If your brain exploded once that number reached double digits, because you just can't imagine ever having the cash or credit to buy that many properties, let me introduce you to your new best friend: creative financing

Creative financing, also known as "no money down real estate", has gotten an unfairly bad rap due to its ubiquitous presence as a late-night TV sales infomercial pitch.[27] Many people assume that because "no money down" is the siren song of so many slightly greasy-looking television pitchmen, it must be just another get rich quick scheme.

But the truth is, low money and no money down deals are done every day by real estate investors, and are actually relatively easy to accomplish in our market once you know how they work and–more importantly–how they can benefit you and your sellers

---

[27] And the fact that it sounds vaguely illegal, like "creative bookkeeping".

59

Just as importantly as the "no money down" aspect of these deals is the "no qualifying" aspect. If your credit is a problem, or you're self-employed, or you don't have 20% down, or you don't have a ton of cash reserves, you're not a very attractive borrower to a bank. In creative finance deals, these 'qualification are really, truly unimportant.

What "Creative Finance" Really Means

Creative finance is a sweeping term that covers any financing terms that are negotiated between two individuals, rather than the individual and an institutional lender. There are no banks or mortgage brokers involved in creative finance deals—it's you and someone else making a deal to finance a piece of propert .

And it's not some new-fangled concept invented by real estate gurus, either. Creative finance is a very, very old and time-honored way to buy real estate. I mean, seriously, how do you think people bought land before banks and mortgages existed? They either paid cash, or they made payments to the owner, or they borrowed the money from someone else and made payments to them. In fact, prior to the establishment of the Federal Housing Administration in the 1930s, there was no such thing as a "bank mortgage" the way we think about it today (relatively low money down, with a 30 year amortization, no balloon), and many American homeowners, landlords, and farmers bought their properties using what we'd now call creative financing[28]

Creative finance deals can be done on any type of real estate. Everything from single family homes to commercial properties to land are bought and sold creatively in our market every week.

Because creative financing is such a catch-all term, it might help you to understand the kinds of forms these transactions take. Creative financing deals that you'll do will fall generally into one of these categories:

---

28 But they probably just called financing

Owner-Held Mortgages, AKA "Seller Carry Backs". Let's say you meet a seller--perhaps an older homeowner or a retiring landlord-- who doesn't owe anything on his property. Could he agree to give you the property and let you pay the purchase price in monthly payments over time? Of course he could. It's perfectly legal, and can be a real win-win for you and the seller.

When a seller does this, the way in which he's protected from your potential non-payment is the same way in which a bank would be protected--he has a formal, written promissory note from you describing how much you owe, what the rate of interest (if any) is on your debt, what the payments will be, when they're due, what the late fee is when they're late, and for how many years the payments will be made. He also has a mortgage recorded at the county, which basically says that if you don't pay the note according to the terms, he can initiate a legal action--foreclosure--to recover the property.

Even a seller who doesn't own his property outright can carry financing by doing a wrap-around mortgage, agreeing to a "take over payments" deal (below) or engaging in one of the other techniques discussed here. However, when a property is free and clear, you should be ready with an offer involving a seller-held mortgage.

Taking Over Existing Financing, AKA "Buying Subject To the Existing Loan". Statistically, only about 20-25% of properties in the U.S. are owned free and clear. That means that the other 75-80% are subject to one or more mortgage liens.

In these cases, it might be to your advantage, and the sellers, to have you "take over" his debt. While this is similar to the formal loan assumptions that we could do on FHA and VA loans prior to 1989, it's different in one key respect: the bank that holds the financing is not typically notified that the property has been sold and that you, not the seller, are now responsible to make the monthly payments.

The reason for this is the "Due on Sale" clause that's present in all conventional, institutional notes today. This clause says that if the seller sells his property, he has to pay off the loan, and if he doesn't, the bank can call the entire balance due and payable immediately, *even if the payments are being made on time and in full.*

Despite this clause, which presents a clear (if not likely to materialize) risk that you, as the buyer, could find yourself in the position of needing to pay off the entire loan at some point in the future, many real estate investors buy many properties this way. Why?

Because taking over someone else's loan is cheaper--there's no requirement for a down payment, no new appraisal, no points, closing costs, or financing fees.

Because the seller's rate of interest might be much lower than what you, as an investor, could get even if you DID qualify for a new loan.

And because you can almost always pay MORE for a property if you have no financing costs, no down payment, and a low monthly payment than if you have to pay cash or get a new loan, and paying more makes sellers happy.

There's a lot to know about buying houses subject to the existing loan--how to write up the contract, disclose all the risks in writing to the seller, protect YOURSELF against future actions of the seller (like if he declares bankruptcy and includes the loan--which, remember, is still in HIS name--in the filing), and more. But it's worth learning about, given that we're coming out of a period where lots of loans were originated at sub-4% interest rates. Taking them over requires some care and knowledge, but might well be worth it if it allows you to buy houses with incredibly low, fixed rate monthly payments

Land Installment Contracts (AKA Contracts For Deed, Agreements For Deed, Bonds For Deed, etc). When a seller is willing to accept payments, but doesn't want to give you the deed to the property, a land contract is often the best solution.

In a land contract, the owner agrees to transfer the deed to you only when the final payment of principle is made. In the meantime, you–although you're not the legal title holder–have all the rights of an owner. The buyer gets to depreciate the property for tax purposes, and can rent, renovate, sell, or otherwise dispose of the property. As the buyer, your interest in the property is reflected in a recorded document at the courthouse.

What's required by a seller and buyer in a land contract is governed primarily by state law, so a land contract document created for a deal in Iowa isn't necessarily applicable in Ohio. When buying on land contract, as when buying with any form of non-traditional financing, make certain that you've had all of the forms, documents, and disclosures created or reviewed by a knowledgeable local attorney.

Lease-Options. Just as you can sell a property you own via a lease with option to buy, you can buy someone else's property on lease/option.

As the "buyer", you are actually in a tenant/landlord relationship with the owner–but, unlike a normal tenant, you have the right to sublease the property to your own tenant or tenant/buyer. Since your purchased price is fixed during the term of the option with the seller, you get the advantage of appreciation–that is, if the property increases in value while you have control over it, you can sell it for more than you owe.

You have a second source of income in the form of cash flo , since you should always negotiate a lower rent payment with the seller than you can get from a tenant. On the other hand, if the property decreases in value or turns out to be more trouble than it's worth, you can simply choose not to exercise your option to buy–and, if your documents are correctly drafted, the only "loss" you should incur will be the amount of the option fee you paid up front.

Private Lenders and Partnerships. Let's face it, not every seller can or will finance his property for you

That's when you turn to other individuals who have money they'd like to invest for a fixed return (private lenders) or who would like to take the higher risk (and reap the higher profits) of partial ownership of a property as a partner.

There are literally hundreds of thousands of these folks in the country today. Some of them are "stock market refugees" who have absolutely no interest in finding, negotiating, fixing or managing real estate, but do have cash that they've divested sitting around in low-yielding accounts that they'd like to invest at higher rates of interest.

Some of them are seasoned real estate investors who are at a point in their careers where they'd like to provide all the money and let you do all the work.

Some of them are people who don't have enough money to buy an entire property, but who have great credit at the 20% down needed to get a bank loan, and who are willing to "lend" you their credit so that you can partner on a deal and get a relatively low, fixed, 30 year rate

And as with other forms of creative finance, you can negotiate the terms to your heart's content–what you pay, and when, and at what rate of interest or what percentage of the deal—is completely a matter of agreement between you and the guy with the money.

So, Who's Going to Do These Deals With Me?

As a real estate entrepreneur who almost certainly wants to buy more deals than you have the cash or credit to do on your own, it's super-easy for you to imagine why YOU want other people to finance properties for you. What might be tougher is understanding why a seller would take payments on their house rather than hold out for a cash offer, or let you take over their payments, or why a private lender or partner would trust you with their cash.

The answer is that **these deals meet some need of the individual seller or money person**. We've already talked about why 3rd party lenders and partners want to do business with you—for the passive returns. But the most common reasons that sellers finance deals for you has less to do with making money on the return than they do with the seller's situation. The main reasons SELLERS finance properties include:

- **You can pay a higher price for their property if they can take that price over time**. If a seller had a property worth $100,000, would you pay $200,000 for it? No? What if the terms were $1 a year for 200,000 years? Silly example, but it shows that there's real value in good terms.

You can close faster if the seller will carry financing. Imagine a seller who's under intense time pressure to get his property sold NOW. Maybe the city is on his back about code violations, and he's got a court date in a week where he's going to get fined $1,500 for not fixing the gutters. Maybe he got a job transfer all the way across the country, needs to move next week, and hasn't sold his house. Maybe he bought a new house and couldn't sell the old one, and can't figure out how he's going to afford both payments next month. A seller in these positions doesn't have the luxury of waiting for a buyer to apply for and get traditional financing, which can take up to 2 months. Your offer of taking the property off his hands in return for monthly payments sounds a whole lot better to a seller like this than waiting around for a cash offer.

- **The seller wants debt relief**. For the seller who owes close to what his home is worth, it can actually COST him money to sell traditionally. By the time he's paid an agent, plus closing costs, plus some expenses on the BUYER'S new loan, he may have to walk into the closing with $5,000 or more cash just to sell his house. If he lets you take over his payments, it might cost him nothing, or just a few hundred dollars.

- **The seller is in a tax situation that makes selling creatively more profitable than selling conventionally**. A seller with a completely depreciated apartment building can expect to pay 20% or more of the sales price of that building in taxes. If he leases it to you with an option to buy, he gets rid of the management of the building and gets monthly payments, but doesn't have to pay the taxes until you exercise your option.

- **Most basically, the seller needs to get rid of the property more than he needs to get cash for it**. It's absolutely true that most sellers want cash (and, for that matter, full price) for their properties. That's because most sellers aren't motivated. They have nice properties in decent areas and aren't under a huge amount of pressure to sell.

In our business—and if you didn't read the chapter on not paying retail, this would be a good time to do that—we're never looking so much for a particular property as we are for a seller with a problem. Sellers with real problems are open to real solutions, even if they involve creative ones, like "Let me take over your loan", or "Take payments instead of all cash".

How Many Properties Could You Buy This Year If

You Understood Creative Finance?

The answer is, as many as you could reasonably handle.

When you understand various creative finance techniques, there is really and truly no reason to invest your own money in any good deal. Between seller financing, private financing, and partners, there are plenty of people out there who want to cooperate with you in getting them the returns they want and/or getting rid of a property they don't want.

For this reason, you'll find that creative finance, in its various forms, is a common topic of discussion and education at our association. In fact, when you attend, you might just find your next partner, lender, or even seller willing to carry back financing

LESSON 5

Know When to Quit (Your Job, That Is)

Maybe you love your job.

Maybe it's in a field you're completely geeked out about, or at a company that has Google-level benefits. Maybe you're in a profession that really helps people, or is your life's calling.

If this is the case, you're probably thinking approaching real estate as a way to make some extra money part-time, or to assure that you have enough income and wealth when you retire to get you through the last 30 or 40 years of your life in style. And if so, that's great, and real estate—wisely evaluated and correctly purchased—can definitely do that for you.

But to be completely honest, most of the people who walk through our doors are looking for total and complete financial independence— the kind that lets you get up tomorrow morning and go to work, or go to Italy, or go back to bed, and still know that you can pay the bills and live well.

And because most people understand that having most jobs is not compatible with total freedom, they're looking for real estate to become their one and only source of income.

In other words, they want to quit their jobs ASAP.

If you grew up in an environment that delivered the message that the right way to live your life—the RESPONSIBLE way—was to have a "real" job, with a pay check every Friday and a 401K and gold watch when you retire, that feeling you have that you and a job just aren't a good fit may cause you some inner conflict. You might feel like you're being selfish for even considering a lifestyle where you don't have to punch a clock or answer to another human being ever again.

If that's the case, consider the fact that, by becoming a full-time real estate entrepreneur, you can do MORE good than you can as a cog in the machine of someone else's business. And that means both for you and your family, AND for the greater community. As a full-time real estate investor, you:

- **Build wealth that will secure the financial future of your family not just in this generation, but indefinitely**. If your children and grandchildren and great-grandchildren play their cards right, they'll never have to depend on an employer, or taxpayers, to support them, because of the estate that YOU'RE building right now.

- **Create jobs for others**. Your team—contractors, professionals, administrative people, and a host of others—all, to some extent, benefit from your business as it provides needed income for THEIR families. You'll also support local jobs and businesses by buying tools and materials, appliances, office equipment, and so on

- **Improve your community**. When you—or, if you're a wholesaler, one of your buyers—take a run down, ugly, unoccupied property and turn it into a livable home, you do more than just make a local neighborhood prettier. You also put it back on the tax rolls as a performing property with a higher value, thus providing property taxes for schools and other local services. You raise the value of the adjoining properties, according to studies, by 7-10%. And perhaps most importantly, you provide decent, affordable housing for a tenant or homeowner who needs it.

- **Build a sense of pride and self-sufficiency in yourself, and become a role model for others**. Sadly, our country is suffering from a serious loss of confidence in our own foundations of freedom and capitalism. More and more Americans are more and more willing to hand over their liberties to the government in return for the promise of cradle-to-grave care. We seem less and less willing to take even the most minor risks in order to get major rewards. When you buck that trend and become a financial success without depending on other taxpayers, you get a sense of pride in yourself that's very deserved, since you built a business that didn't exist before. You also stand in front of your family, friends, and colleagues as living proof that, with desire and hard work, it's still possible to go from rags to riches in America today.

Having said this, many people struggle with the decision about when to leave the relative security of a full-time job in favor of a life of self-unemployment. Some jump the gun, and give notice after their first successful deal. Others continue to work at a job they hate for years beyond the time when it's no longer necessary.

So when is the right time? It varies from person to person based on their situations and risk tolerance. But here are some clues that it may be time to kiss your job goodbye:

- **You're making more per hour for the hours you spend on your real estate business than you are on your job.** I recently spoke to a relatively new investor who'd wholesaled 3 or 4 properties over the course of the last year for an average profit of $7,000 each. Each deal had taken him less and less time to complete, and his hourly "wage" on his last deal had worked out to about $500 per hour. He quit his full-time, $60,000-a-year job because he realized that he could replace the income from it working just 120 hours a year. Another

20 hours would pay the taxes due from his deals and replace his medical insurance, as well. And an additional 10 hours would take care of the matching funds his employer was putting into his 401-K annually. Trading a 2,000 hour a year job for a 150 hour a year job at the same salary just made sense to him–and he had enough deals under his belt to be confident that he could repeat these results over and ove .

- **Your 'real job' is getting in the way of your real estate business**. This same investor felt that he had lost more potential deals than he had made by being unavailable to take calls from potential sellers during the day and by being limited to viewing properties to evenings and weekends. A close friend of mine experienced a similar situation–after almost 20 years in corporate America, she realized that she was taking all of her vacation and sick days to oversee renovations on her collection of 10 properties, and decided that she could acquire and renovate 2-3 times as many properties if not for her time commitments to work. So when the next round of layoffs came, she volunteered to take the severance package, and got busy building her holdings to the point that they would support her.

- **You aren't making as much from your real estate as you are from your salary, but it's not costing you as much, either**. When my father "retired" from his job as vice president of an engineering firm at the age of 40, it was afte making this calculation:
  - My apartment buildings produce a pre-tax income of $29,000 per year
  - My job pays $39,000 per year with benefits and bonus (this was 1976, by the way) However, my job COSTS me
  - $2,000 per year in expensive work clothing and dry-cleaning, which I won't need anymore
  - $1,500 more per year in lunches eaten at restaurants than

I'd pay to eat at home

- $1,000 per year in gas and wear and tear on my car getting to and from work
- $1,500 in unreimbursed travel expenses–magazines at the airport, tips to the bellman at the hotel and the skycap, etc.
- $3,500 in income taxes (he paid no taxes on his rental income, thanks to depreciation)
- $1,000 in miscellaneous gifts, donations, etc. expected at a large offic

In short, my job actually pays more than $500 LESS per year than my apartment buildings. Thus, I need to quit my job and buy more property. And that's what he did.

- **Your job is wreaking so much havoc on your mental health or family life** that your choices are: go crazy, get divorced, or alienate your kids forever; quit and have no income; or quit and give the real estate thing a try. This is a risky proposition, but sometimes desperation is a great motivator. And worst case scenario, you can always get another job if real estate doesn't do it for you.

Quitting your job is a very personal decision. It's always scary–but it's also exciting, fulfilling, and fun. Let your brain, rather than your fears, guide you in the decision about when to leave that job behind and jump full-time into real estate investing.

LESSON 6

Pay Attention or Pay Big: Asset Protection for Beginners

At the next Association meeting, ask the active investors you meet what kind of entity they operate under.

Then, let it tell you something that every single one of them either has an answer ("I have an LLC", "I use Limited Partnerships", and so on), or is very aware that they SHOULD have an answer ("I know I need to get an LLC").

There are two good reasons that successful investors own properties and flip deals through entities: the first (and actually most important) is that properly-formed and managed entities can literally make you thousands of dollars a year by reducing the amount of income tax you pay on the money you make.

The second is that properly-formed and managed entities can protect your hard-won real estate empire from a very real threat in this country today: the threat of losing everything you own to a nuisance lawsuit, a jackpot jury verdict, or some other legal "lightning strike" that you can't predict nor control.

Now, you may be thinking, "Only bad guys get sued, and even if the occasional good guy like myself accidentally winds up in court, I'll win, 'cause I'm good. And even if I don't, I'll have insurance to cover me. Asset protection is for bad guys and paranoid people".

If only.

The reality is, you'll need to create and run your business through an entity—probably a Limited Liability Company, but possibly something else, depending on your own situation—as soon as it's practically possible. Why? Let me count the ways:

- *When you own investment real estate, many people assume that you must be rich. And sadly, that attracts financial predators.* You may not FEEL rich, because that $100,000 rental house has an $80,000 mortgage on it and is only clearing $100 a month. But the fact is, many Americans don't even own <u>one</u> house, and here you are, the owner of 2, or 3, or 10. In the eyes of certain folks, that means you MUST have some seriously deep pockets.

  And unfortunately, there's a small but growing part of the population that finds filing lawsuits against "rich" people t be an easy and profitable way of making a living. You've seen them on T.V.—they're the same people who stage slip-and-falls in grocery stores hoping to collect a $20,000 settlement.

  Does it seem impossible that lil' ol' you will ever become the victim of such a financial predator? Then go ahead—own a bunch of properties in your own name, and see what happens. Or, just skip that stage and learn from the generation of real estate entrepreneurs before you. Basically, any owner of investment real estate who's owned enough of it for long enough has been the victim of one of these nuisance lawsuits or financial predators. And one reason that real estate is particularly subject to this kind of action is that…

- *Unlike "soft" assets like bank accounts, cash, stocks, antiques, etc, real estate ownership is public record.* It's literally possible to discover every single piece of property that an individual owns simply by going online and entering their name into a government website. This is both a handy tool for bad guys who are looking for someone with proverbial "deep pockets" AND a way for someone who's already taken it into their head to sue you for slights or damages, real or imagined, to determine what else you might have that they could get.

Now, the reality is that the first thing a potential plainti f will do is contact an attorney. The first thing the ATTORNEY will do is to determine whether he thinks the case is winnable and, if so, if you're likely to be able to pay up. If the mental, physical, or financial injury to his client is something that insurance would typically cover—like a broken bone from a fall on your property—the attorney will almost certainly take the case on contingency (meaning that the plaintiff doesn't have to pay unless he wins the case). If the injury is NOT something that insurance would cover (see that list below) and it at least appears that you have relatively few assets with which to satisfy any judgment or settlement, he's likely to ask the plaintiff for a retainer–which stops most nuisance suits dead in their tracks

Certain types of asset protection offer you "privacy" in the sense that no immediate connection can be made between you and all the properties you own, or even between those properties themselves. This can make you a much less attractive target for nuisance cases—especially those that are far-fetched or those that are of a nature that insurance would typically not cover. Speaking of which…

• *There is a long and growing list of risks against which no property insurance will insure.* If you're still thinking, "Let 'em sue! I have great insurance!", think again. Many of the things you can get covered by your homeowner's policy are literally impossible to get covered in your "non-owner occupied" policy. If you lose a claim for one of these things, the judgment has to be paid by you, as does your legal defense to begin with. For example, the insurance policy on your rental property will almost certainly not cover:

- Damages from most types of "environmental toxins", including mold, lead paint, radon, and asbestos
- Claims of fair housing violations
- Dog bites or injuries from certain breeds of dog your tenant might have, including Pitt Bulls, Chows, German Shepherds, Rottweilers, and mixes of any of the above
- Damage to your tenants' possessions because of fire, floo or other, otherwise insurable risks

  And, don't forget—insurance policies have liability limits. If you have a million dollar liability limit and a jury hands down a $3 million judgment against you, guess who gets to pay?

- *The US graduates more new lawyers each year than the rest of the world combined.* And all these well-scrubbed, enthusiastic new lawyers need to find a way to make a living So they actively market to potential plaintiffs asking them to think really, really hard about whom in their lives might have treated them wrong and therefore need to be sued. You've seen proof of it if you've ever watched daytime T.V., which seems to be supported primarily by attorneys drumming up business by soliciting calls from everyone whose ever used this drug or gotten that implant.
  And guess what—it's ever cheaper and easier for these folks to reach your tenants, via the U.S. Postal service!
  One enterprising firm in Pennsylvania has, in recent years engaged in a multi-state mailing campaign to tenants in

older neighborhoods explaining that if their children are doing poorly in school, are acting up, or ever get sick to their stomachs or seem listless that the problem is probably lead paint in their rental homes. They then offer a free medical consultation and a toll free number to call in case the tenant would like to get one of the multi-million dollar settlements this firm has gotten from landlords all over the country. This is, of course, at no cost to the tenant unless the firm achieves a settlement. If you'd like to get a taste of the amount of sheer volume of these sorts of pitches, go to any internet search engine and type in "landlord+sue" or "property+owner+lawsuit".

- *Yes, you're a really good person. Except that as the "rich", successful landlord or investor, you are always the bad guy.* Whether in front of a jury, a housing court, or a regulating agency such as the local building department or neighborhood association, the assumption is always made that, as a landlord, you have a vested interest in making money at any cost. Don't believe me? Ask any ten of your non-investor friends what they think of landlords in general. Then imagine them as ten of your peers, sitting in a jury box, and think of the entrenched prejudices against landlords and real estate investors you'll have to overcome if you're ever sued.

So How Can Asset Protection Help?

The point of all of this is simply to show you that owning investment properties carries risks that can cost you a lot more than the money you have invested in the properties themselves. In fact, unless you have appropriate asset protection in place, a single million-plus dollar judgment can wipe out not only your entire real estate portfolio, but also your own home, banks and investment accounts, as well.

Luckily, there are ways to legally separate your assets from one another, so that even if something unexpected happens, only part of what you've built will be at risk.

When properly set up and maintained, each entity is effectively a separate "artificial person" that owns its own set of properties. If something goes wrong with one of the properties that this "person" owns, only the other properties and assets owned by that entity are at risk.

For instance, let's imagine that you own 30 properties in your own name, representing $3 million in assets. In one property, a tenant's guest falls down the stairs and breaks his back. After a long, stressful trial, the guest is awarded a $4 million judgment–$3 million more than the cap on your liability policy. The opposing attorney certified the judgment, and then proceeds to foreclose on and auction off your entire empire. End of story.

One of COREE's founders is nationally-known asset protection and tax expert John Hyre. If you're suddenly realizing that the assets you already have are at risk, you might want to contact him via his website, www.RealEstateTaxLaw.com

On the other hand, if your 30 properties are divided among 3 Limited Liability Companies (LLCs), each of which has $1 million in net assets, the tale ends a bit differently. Although the plaintiff's attorney will try to name you personally in the case, he will probably fail; therefore, only the actual owner–your LLC–will be a defendant. Again, the jury awards a $4 million verdict. But this time, there is only $1 million in assets to satisfy the judgment, leaving you with $2 million to start over with. And if the 30 properties are divided among 10 LLCs with just $300,000 in assets each...you get the picture.

Incidentally, placing your properties in LLCs, Limited Partnerships, Corporations, and Trusts that you, in turn, own may serve a second purpose–it hides your overall financial picture and makes you a less attractive target for true "nuisance" lawsuits.

An attorney debating whether or not to take a weak case—especially one that would probably not be settled by your insurance company--will always look into the public record to see how much equity is available to satisfy a potential judgment. If he sees that you are the owner of 30 properties, he's likely to go forward; if he sees that the owner is a trust with only one other property, he's likely to give it a pass.

And if the risk of losing everything you ever worked for isn't enough to convince you that you need an entity, here's a final thought: a properly selected and managed entity can save you thousands of dollars a year in taxes. It's a topic that's worth studying, and one that you'll find frequently discussed at our association

How and When It's OK to Involve Your Loved Ones in Your Business

On the one hand, the love and support of your significant other, immediate family, and close friends are important to your success in the scary new venture of investing in real estate.

In fact, a big part of the reason you want to be rich probably has to do with being able to do things for and with your family. Your goal may be to make sure your children or grandchildren can get the best possible education, or to see that your aging parents get the best care available, or to support a handicapped relative, or to buy your mom a house of her own. You may want to start a business that you can work in with your spouse and kids. You may simply want the freedom to be a "stay at home" parent.

And those are all admirable (and attainable) goals. But at the same time, you need to realize that the very people that you want to help may not be as supportive of your burning desire to better yourself as you'd imagine.

In fact, just to warn you, **it's pretty common for a lot of the people in your life to be dead-set against your real estate endeavors**.

There are a lot of reasons for this—and most of them have to do with their own fears and concerns. Here are some common ones we've heard:

- Your bosses and colleagues are worried that your real estate activities will cause you to be less "present" at work, and they'll have to pick up the slack. Plus, maybe they're a little jealous that you're doing something that will significantly reduce your reliance on a paycheck, and they're not.

- Your friends all have cautionary tales about people THEY know who lost a bunch of money in real estate, and constantly feel obligated to "warn" you about all the things they've heard about real estate. Plus, maybe they're a little worried that you WILL get rich, and then you'll get new, rich friends.

- Your parents, who worked nice, secure W-2 jobs their entire lives, think you're irresponsible for even THINKING about giving up a "secure paycheck"[29] and an employer 401K contribution

- Your spouse is significantly more risk-averse than you are, and thinks you're going to drive the family into bankruptcy by agreeing to pay even "good debt" that generates income

- Your kids are worried about losing your time (though they'll rarely admit it), and act out by being snide, or ignoring you, or wearing their jeans around their knees to get your "attention".

It's easy to think, "Well, I'm just so determined that it doesn't really matter what anyone else says—I'll just shrug it off and not let it affect me". Which is fine, until the time that you're facing your own doubts because it's been 3 weeks and you haven't closed a deal yet, and you're getting the constant message from people you care about that you can't, or shouldn't, or won't, do this whole real estate thing.

The reality, it's REALLY hard to hear over and over and over again that you're going to fail, or that you shouldn't even try, or that your loved ones don't support you, and still press forward with what you need to do.

---

29 Whatever THAT means, in America today

So you need to be prepared for the inevitability that SOMEONE whose opinion you value is going to try to discourage you, and take these steps to succeed anyway:

1. Be VERY careful about the people with whom you share your goals in the first place. You're going to be sooooo excited when you start learning about all the money-making possibilities in real estate. You're going to be even MORE excited when you get your first deal under contract, and when you get your first big fat check, and when you finish your first rehab, or when you buy your first rental. In fact, it will be almost irresistible to tell everyone who will listen about how amped you are.

But you SHOULD resist sharing your dreams and successes with certain people—and if you don't know which ones right now, you will once you start.

Anyone in your life who's just a critical person, anyone who doesn't have your best interests at heart, anyone who's the "jealous type", is likely to discourage you ("I read that real estate investing doesn't work here"), criticize you ("You're looking for houses in THAT neighborhood? I wouldn't drive through THAT neighborhood with my doors locked!") or belittle you ("Isn't that cute? She can't meet a deadline at work, but she thinks she's going to be a real estate mogul!"). Don't give them the chance to bring you down—you'll need every bit of your determination and optimism to succeed.

2. Make sure the people you NEED in your corner are educated. It's not a bit unusual for one significant other in a relationship to be a lot more risk averse or fearful than the other. And when yours doesn't understand WHY it's not a huge risk to agree to a $100,000 loan on a $150,000 property[30], it's a lot harder for him or her to support what you're doing.

---

30   Especially when that loan doesn't have your personal signature on it

And YOU might not be the right person to explain the financial and legal ramific tions of any given action. You're SO might need to hear these things from a 3rd party expert. So taking your partner to at least a basic level workshops or seminars is a good idea. Including him or her in meetings with your mentor, lender, agent, attorney, and so on allows him to ask the questions that are preying on his mind directly, rather than having them filtered through you.

Ultimately, some families end up having to implement a "don't ask, don't tell" policy where it comes to one partner's real estate activities. If someone you care a lot about—be it a romantic partner, parent, or even close friend—simply can't get past the fear or insecurity or jealously or whatever it is that triggers him to launch into a list of reasons that what you're doing won't work, or why you personally can't succeed at it, you may simply have to put your foot down and force an agreement that you won't worry them by talking about deals you're doing, and they won't hassle you by talking about how you're bound to fail.

3. **Never listen to the advice of anyone who's making less money in real estate than you are**. It never ceases to amaze me how people who've never bought a piece of investment real estate—or who bought just one, and that was 15 years ago—are just full of wisdom about what you should and, more importantly, shouldn't do. And why would you take one bit of that to heart? Unless the advice-giver has broad,

---

Bonus Tip: Join COREE to Get the Positive Feedback You Need.

It's not enough to avoid the nay-sayers: you have to have yay-sayers in your life, too! No matter how long you've been investing in real estate or how many successes you've had, it's still awesome to get together with a group of like-minded people to get the support, encouragement, and congratulations you need to get through the discouraging times and celebrate the wins.

experienced-based knowledge to share, hum a little tune to yourself while they're talking and think about that cute kitten you saw on YouTube this morning until they're finished.

4. **Bringing home a big check is the best proof of concept**. Honestly, there may be some people in your life that are so jealous and small-minded that you'll never hear the end of the jabs about your 'little side business', even after you've been in real estate full time for decades.

But in the case of most of the critics, the thing that will shut them up, and fast, is when you actually do what you set out to do. Try not to rub it in the faces of the people who didn't believe in you when you bring home your first big check from a deal. But don t try too hard.

Doing Business with Friends and Family

One other warning about friends and family: don't bring them into your business without a great deal of forethought, discussion, and legal documentation.

And when I say "bring them into your business", I mean in any form—as partners, employees, tenants, lenders, buyers, contractors. These arrangements are infamous in the real estate world for souring (or ending altogether) formerly close relationships.

Whatever the details of the situation, the root cause is always the same: you and your friend go into the deal with different expectations, but you both think that the other knows what's going on.

For instance, you might have the deal-making experience and the money, and you know that your brother is a great renovator. You figure that he knows that getting the deal you've bought together is top priority; he thinks you understand that he has to take outside jobs that will get him a check at the end of THIS WEEK first. Your money sits in your deal for months while he works on other people's houses. You get mad; he gets defensive. Next thing you know, Thanksgiving dinner is an uncomfortable ordeal for everyone involved.

As in any business, getting involved in real estate with people you know is risky. Never, never place someone you care about in the position of costing you money unless your agreement is outlined in writing. And be sure to include "worst case scenario" agreements that specify how the property will be disposed of if one or both parties decide it's too much work, or not enough profit, or just too stressful to deal with.

For the Educated Entrepreneur, There's No Such Thing as a "Bad" Real Estate Market

If you had a time machine, and you could only use it to choose a year in which to start investing in real estate, which year would you choose?

Would it be 2001, before the huge run-up in prices took hold, so you could buy some properties cheaply and sell them before the crash? Because if so, you'd be buying houses in the middle of a recession, and you'd need to have a plan that would allow you to hold onto them until the economy recovered.

Would it be 2006, when you could wholesale houses in a matter of days for 5-figure profits, and have buyers fighting over them? If that's the plan, better bring a lot of marketing money along, because the super-hot market also meant that there was a lot of competition for good deals.

Would it be 2009, when properties were literally selling for the fabled 'pennies on the dollar'? Because if you chose that date, you'd better be prepared to pay cash or have a bunch of private financing there'd be no institutional financing available for you to pay for all those bargains. Oh, and I wouldn't plan to sell them right away, because that financing wasn't available for ANYONE, including highly qualified homeowners and investors. Ask me how I know.

When the media talks about "good" markets and "bad" markets, it tends to focus on just one perspective, and that's the perspective of the seller of a piece of residential real estate. A "good" market, if you believe the nightly news, is one in which house prices are increasing and sales are brisk.

Which is a metric you'd probably agree with if you're trying to sell your home or your rehab in that market, or you're a real estate agent or a mortgage broker or a builder who makes more money when more people are buying.

On the other hand, if you're a first-time homebuyer on a limited budget who keeps getting outbid on house after house that you want to buy, you might not think such a market was so "good". Or if you're a landlord with a bread-and-butter house that just won't rent because all the qualifi d renters are buying homes instead, you might just curse that "good" market. Or if you're an investor in self-storage units, which actually tend to do BETTER when people are renting rather than buying, you'll probably just brace yourself for the "good" market and prepare to ride it out until the "bad" market—which is actually the better market for you—comes back.

As a residential real estate entrepreneur, you are always, at some level, in the business of providing housing. And the awesome thing about housing is, it's literally always in demand. It doesn't matter what's going on in the economy—human beings still need a place to live. Sure, if the worst happens, they may live 10 to a house, or they may move to more affordable properties in not-so-nice areas, but they WILL put a roof over their heads, no matter what.

Thus, there is always a market for what you have to sell. The NATURE of the demand shifts—from rental housing to purchases and back again, from easy institutional financing to more owner financing and back again, and so on—but the market is always there.

The point is, "good" and "bad" markets mean something completely different to you as a real estate entrepreneur than they do to home owners, or agents, or the general public. The ONLY thing you need to know to make money when the rest of the world has pulled the metaphorical blankets over its metaphorical head so that it can mean and groan over how "bad" things are can be stated in two sentences:

1. Buy when others are selling, and sell when others are buying
2. Shift your exit strategy to meet the demand of the moment, and be ready to shift it again when that demand, inevitably, changes

The Houston market is a case-in-point. During the crash of the oil industry in the 80s, housing in Houston took a major hit. Entire subdivision sat empty; foreclosed properties where everywhere; sellers often found that their mortgage balances were significantly more than what the few remaining buyers were willing to pay. Home prices in some neighborhoods dropped by 50% or more seemingly overnight.

Needless to say, the not too many real estate entrepreneurs were excited about doing business in Houston during this period. The wholesale real estate market depends on retailer and landlord buyers; the retailers largely closed up shop because THEY had no buyers, and many of the landlords went into "survival mode", trying to figure out how to deal with their existing rentals, which they suddenly found themselves "upside down" in.

But the real pros, who'd educated themselves about borrowing private money, and multiple exit strategies, and who had the intestinal fortitude to simply believe that this was just another (fairly extreme) market cycle, did exactly the opposite: they bought and bought and bought.

What's the best way to keep track of what's happening in the Central Ohio Market? You guessed it—join COREE and COME TO MEETINGS. The media and the public always spot trends MONTHS after our members, who are on the ground buying, selling, and renting properties on a day to day basis, do. In a changing market, knowledge isn't just power—it's money. And since our market is moving all the time, our community at COREE is a big part of your ability to move with it—and your confidence that you're doing the right thing, no matter what outsiders are telling you.

In fact, one Houston-area entrepreneur I know found an entire subdivision of nearly 100 properties that was 2/3rds finished, but which had never been occupied. He got some money backers, bought the entire subdivision from the bankruptcy court at under $10,000 per 3-bedroom house, and rented them all at an under-market rent of $400 per month. Using the positive cash flo , he finished the 30 or so properties that had been abandoned in some stage of construction, and then just—waited.

As the market slowly recovered through the early and mid-90s, he began to sell off the now 5 year old houses. The first ones sold in the $55,000 range. As the market heated up, he was able to sell in the $60s, then the $70s. By the end of the project 10 years later, he was able to sell of the remaining buildable lots for $15,000 each—more than he'd paid for the houses themselves a decade earlier.

This project made this investor—and his money partners—multi-millionaires over the course of a decade.

Was it a risky endeavor to buy so many houses in a down market? In retrospect, it's easy for us to say, "Nah, he was able to make money holding them, so even if the market never recovered, he'd just collect the cash flow forever and ever and he'd be fine." But although he now tells the story as if he knew that making millions was a foregone conclusion, I'm sure that at the time, it was a scary thing to do.

It's human nature to follow the herd, and to be affected by other people's attitudes about the real estate market or any other market.

But after more than a quarter century of buying, selling, renting, and financing real estate in "good" markets and "bad" markets, I'm here to tell you that there is lots and lots of money to be made in EVERY market.

The key is to stay aware of what's happening in OUR market. Are more people selling than buying? Then round up some money and buy at rock bottom prices. Are more people buying than selling? Offload some of that cheap inventory you got at the bottom of the market, at the new higher prices. Is there a lot of rental demand? Rent, or sell houses to people who do and who don't have enough properties to fulfill the demand.

Ask any association member who made their fortune AFTER the market 'crashed' in 2007-2008, or because of the recession in 2001, or during the early 80s, when interest rates were 15% and the only real way to buy a house was with owner financing. They'll all tell you that every market is a 'good' market, if YOU know how to best position yourself to take advantage of it.

You WILL Get Educated. Oh Yes, You Will. Here's How to Do it Without Going Broke.

If you want to make safe, profitable real estate deals, there's more you need to know than can be crammed into 100 pages.

And if you've been exploring the real estate education world, you already know that there are endless gurus and infomarketers who are more than willing to accept thousands, or tens of thousands, of dollars of your hard-earned money in return for filling you in on the details of their favorite strategies.

But before you spend as much on a real estate "education" as it costs to buy a cheap house in our area, let me fill you in on the realities of the education biz, and how to navigate it to get the knowledge you need without re-mortgaging your house to get it.

First of all, I'll reiterate that your real estate education is a necessary and high-leverage investment. The bottom line is, you WILL learn the lessons that every successful real estate entrepreneur knows. The question is, will you do it the easy, cheap way, or the hard, expensive way?

The difficult and costly way is to let the market teach you what you need to know. Go ahead, overpay for a house, underestimate the repair costs, put it up for sale and lose $10,000 when you sell it—I promise you you'll learn valuable lessons and you won't repeat the same mistakes twice.

On the other hand, for about 1/5th the cost of that mistake, you could just take a good, complete 4-day course on how to evaluate and rehab properties from someone who's already gone through that process over and over and over, and MAKE money on your next rehab.

The worst way to learn how to be an effective landlord is to let your tenants teach you. The worst way to find out how to wholesale houses is to just run out and do it, and ruin your reputation among serious buyers by offering a bunch of bad deals while you're learning what a good deal looks like.

EVERYONE, and I do mean everyone, who becomes successful in real estate does so by using the hard-won experience of others—be they educators, colleagues, or mentors—who've worked out the kinks in the system and learned how to minimize the risks, avoid the mistakes, and do the thing you're trying to do in the fastest, easiest manner possible.

People who try to avoid spending money to make money end up spending MORE money cleaning up their own messes than they would have by just getting the right information to start with.

At the same time, not all real estate education is created equal. In fact, not to put too fine a point on it, some of the available "education" out there just plain sucks.

A shocking number of the "programs", courses, bootcamps, seminars, and so on aren't worth the paper they're printed on—and yes, I'm including some of those that are completely delivered online.

I own more than $200,000 worth of real estate education myself, and I personally evaluate 40-50 new books, home study courses, and live events each and every year. And I'm here to tell you that a slick sales pitch, a convincing webinar, an awesome offer, or dozens of testimonials from "successful students" absolutely do NOT reflect the quality or quantity of education you get when you invest in a particular piece of education. Much of what I see—and remember, when I say "see", I mean fully read/watch/listen to—is absolutely not worth the money that's being charged for it. Most commonly, the reasons are:

- **The self-proclaimed "guru" simply doesn't have the knowledge or experience to really teach what he's trying to teach**. You might be surprised to find out that some cours promoters claim experience they don't have (one common trick is to say "My partners and I have done over 1 zillion deals" when in fact, he's done 10 and is taking credit for every deal every one of his students have done, even when the students did the deals DESPITE, rather than because of, the teacher's advice). Real estate education is a big-money business; too many of the practitioners make their money selling courses rather than doing the thing they're claiming to teach.

- **The information is incomplete or incomprehensible**. There are real estate instructors out there who are very good at their strategies, but who reach their level of incompetence when they sit down to organize a step-by-step system for showing other people how to do it. Many courses lack the detail you'd need to actually implement the strategy in question; others are so poorly written or organized that you simply can't follow them.

- **The information is outdated**. Some strategies, like rental management, change very little over time. Others, like buying short sales, shift significantly enough from one year to th next that a course produced last year isn't entirely relevant this year. Creating a product is a long and arduous process, and most educators dread the necessary updates so much that they just don't do them.

- **The information isn't intended to "teach" you anything at all**—just to convince you that you need to spend a lot more money on the next, much more expensive step in your education. This is the business model behind the "free" books and reports[31] the $300 entry-level weekend seminars, and other very low-cost education that claims to teach you "everything you need to know about _____". What you learn is just enough to know that you need to buy their very expensive up sell program to know enough to actually do anything.

Don't get me wrong, the cheap overview education definitely has its place when done correctly. If what you're getting is a real overview, not a 3 day long sales pitch or 50 pages of pictures of the kinds of checks you could be taking home if you just spent the money to take the next course, it can be very valuable in helping you understand whether a particular strategy is even something you should think about pursuing.[32] What bothers me is when the "free" or "cheap" education isn't education at all, but pure sales pitch.

The cost of a particular course is not a measure of how complete, realistic, or usable it is. The real estate informarketing business discovered a long time ago that people buy courses and seminars based on emotions—excitement, greed, fear of loss, and so on—rather than on logical evaluation of the actual value of the information. Thus, the

---

[31] That's right, you caught me. But what I'm trying to sell you is a $197, year-long association membership that will change your life, not a $25,000 mentoring program that will just change your credit score.

[32] In fact, one of my favorite types of events to attend is "dog and pony shows", where a dozen or more speakers each get 90-120 minutes to explain and pitch their strategies. It's a great way to get exposed to a lot of new ideas in a short period of time. OREIA happens to hold the best and largest in the country each November; you can get more info at OREIAConvention.com

---

Look What Others are Saying About COREE:

"I can summarize the value of COREE in two words: Education and Networking. I have learned dozens of creative techniques and tips that helped to significantly improve the performance of my rental portfolio and increase the profitability of my deals

I have completed several profitable win-win deals with various COREE members. I would never even have known about these great deals if I had not attended the COREE meetings.

The top shelf education, combined with the opportunity to network with positive, like-minded people who see the benefits and fun of owning and controlling real estate is invaluable. I leave every COREE meeting highly energized and motivated! COREE rocks!!!"—Dave Peters

"My rehab funding company has been involved in several real estate investor groups in Central Ohio, but COREE is the best. It delivers quality educational speakers and workshops at low cost. Besides national speakers, COREE taps local experts to educate the group and is also careful to listen to what the members want to experience on a monthly and annual basis. I have enjoyed my membership and have gained business because of it." –Chris Knoppe, Investment Director at Autumnwood Funding

"COREE brought my passion for real estate back and is continually making a difference in my business. I have met great and knowledgeable individuals. Recently they helped me assess what sounded like a good deal and with their help we correctly evaluated and prevented me from making a costly mistake."— Marianna Dulkina

rule is not that the better the education is, the more it costs; it's that the better the pitch, the more the education costs.

You've probably seen excellent real estate education that costs a few hundred dollars and excellent education that costs $10,000. But you've also seen terrible education at both price points. The trick is that no matter how cynical or sales pitch-immune you think you are, you probably can't tell the difference until you've already spent the money. And no, I'm not insulting your intelligence—I'm just telling you that good pitchmen are really, really good.

Which is why our association spends so much time vetting education FOR you. COREE doesn't exist in a vacuum. We're members of several national associations of real estate groups and group leaders. Our members and leaders attend workshops, web classes, and other events by the hundreds each year. We have a pretty good idea which speakers are "for real" and which are full of it. We know which courses are worth buying and which bootcamps are worth a trip out of town. If you see someone selling on OUR stage, it's because we truly believe that they are not only experienced, knowledgeable, and able to teach, but that they're one of the best in the business.

And if we're wrong, anything you buy at COREE—including membership itself—comes with a 100% satisfaction guarantee. You have 30 days after your purchase to determine that it's quality education that will work for you. If not, you simply return it for a full refund within the 30 day period. That's how confident we are that your investment in the education we bring you is a good one.

Finally, the most proven, time-tested way to get the education you need is to combine education from the right experts with LOCAL knowledge and resources. And no, I'm not just saying this because COREE rocks. I've said this to real estate associations all over the United States, whether I had anything to do with that association or not, because it's true.

Look What Others are Saying About COREE:

"COREE brought my passion for real estate back and is continually making a difference in my business. I have met so great and knowledgeable individuals. Recently they helped me assess what sounded like a good deal and with their help I was able to correctly evaluate it and avoid making a costly mistake."—Marianna Dulkina, COREE member

"I've been to hundreds of real estate associations all over the United States over the past 20 years, and very few of them provide the level of value to their members that COREE does. Dollar for dollar, it's the best investment any real estate entrepreneur can make in their businesses. If you live in the Greater Columbus area and you're in real estate or want to be, you're insane if you don't join this group"—Ron Legrand, Author of "Fast Cash in Quick Turn Real Estate"

ALL successful real estate entrepreneurs have invested in education from other successful entrepreneurs who are experts in their field

The problem is, when your favorite rehab guru lives in Las Vegas, and teaches you all the tips and tricks for finding, financing, renovating, and selling properties for big cash profits, you still have to come home and find the right contractors HERE. To know which neighborhoods HERE are the right ones for the strategy. To get the right agent, title company, and attorney HERE.

Access to that kind of local information and knowledge is just one of the many ways in which COREE membership benefits you. For just $197 per year, you get the LOCAL education, networking, resource sharing, motivation, support and community you need to build the wealth and income in real estate investing you want.

Do yourself the biggest favor you've ever done for your financial future; check out a COREE meeting right away. There's even a pass to attend your first meeting for free on the next page or downloadable at: CentralOhioREIA.com.

We know that when you see all the COREE has to offer, you'll join our community and get what you need to get rich in Central Ohio real estate.

This Pass Entitles the Bearer and Up to Two Guests To One Regular Meeting of The Central Ohio Real Estate Entrepreneurs (COREE) At No Charge

Regular meetings are held the 1st Tuesday of each month 6-9 PM in Columbus.

Location and meeting topics available at www.CentralOhioREIA. com

One per customer, please. Regular guest fee is $30 per meeting.

Interested in Passive Real Estate Investments?

Don't Even THINK About Writing a Check Until You've

Taken Advantage of this FREE Passive Investment Education!

After 25 years in the real estate investing business, I've seen far too many private lenders, partners, and other passive investors get into money-losing deals, for the simple reason that they don't know how to evaluate the opportunities, the paperwork, or the documents, due diligence, and insurance that SHOULD be in place for their protection.

That's why I created a 5-part, free online training for people considering passive real estate investments. You'll learn:

- How to evaluate private lending and partnership deals, performing mortgages, turnkey rentals, and private equity funds

- What you need in place to protect yourself

- How to make passive investments tax-free in your IRA

- What to look for, and what to look OUT for, in your partners

- And much more.

Get this free training at www.REGoddess.com

Want Even More?
Get 30 Days of Training and One-on-One Support for Just

(wait for it…)

$1 The Real Life Real Estate Inner Circle Program

The Missing Link in Your Real Estate Success Chain—

**Email coaching and continuing education at an incredibly affordable price,
with no long-term commitment!**

And Now (For a Limited Time Only)

You Can Try Out All the Amazing Coaching, Education, and Support

YOU Need to Build Your Real Estate Business

for Just $1

(and you can quit anytime, but you won't want to…)

Dear Real Estate Entrepreneur;

Why Aren't <u>You</u> Getting Embarrassingly Rich

in the HOTTEST, Easiest-to-Navigate Real Estate Market in History?

I mean, look around you.

I bet you see tons of people making money and doing deals that are, not to put too fine a point on it, a lot stupider than you are

And I bet you've done all the right things—bought the homestudy courses, attended the seminars and bootcamps, joined your local real estate association...

But There's Still Something Crucial Missing, And

I Know What it is.

My name is Vena Jones-Cox, and I've been buying, selling, financing, and renting properties for over 25 years

I've made money in up markets and down markets; buyer's markets and seller's markets; markets where getting financing was as easy as fogging a mirror and as hard as scaling Mt. Everest without a Sherpa.

I've also been teaching real estate entrepreneurs to create and build profitable businesses for over a decade through non-profit real estate investor associations and my own seminars and courses.

It's because of all this personal and teaching experience that I know exactly what it is that's stopping you from creating complete and total financial independence

You Don't Have the Support You Need to

Make "Rich" Happen for You!

I amazed at the number of budding and even experienced real estate entrepreneurs I meet that believe that every successful investor around them is a self-made millionaire.

I've never actually met a "self-made" millionaire.

I know I'm not one.

If I had had to "go it alone", I would never, ever have found the courage to make my first o fer…

…much less the resources to finance it, get it fixed, or get that first big check in my pocket.

See, here's the big secret EVERY real estate guru, group leader, and millionaire knows, but no one talks about:

Education is Crucial to Real Estate Success—

But it's Not Enough. Ever. For Anyone.

To make money in the real estate business, you HAVE to learn your craft.

It's soooooooo easy to make big mistakes when you're reinventing the wheel—in fact, my guess is that 99% of budding real estate entrepreneurs who try to "learn by doing", without so much as a homestudy course to guide them, lose money on their first few deals

So yes, you've done the right thing by socking away all that information in your brain.

But although there are some awesome manuals, CDs, and seminars out there (and some really bad ones, too), the fact is that:

No matter how thoroughly you've been educated,

No matter how obsessively detailed the instruction,

And no matter how smart or determined YOU are

You simply can't succeed without ongoing support, encouragement, and study.

I've seen it over and over again...

You attend a workshop or read a book.

You get it. You understand what you're supposed to do and how to do it.

You go out in the world to do it...

And you get completely STUCK.

You can't actually "do" the deal, because you have questions that your education didn't—in fact, COULDN'T—answer.

Questions like:

- Have I evaluated this particular deal right?
- Have I thought through all the pros and cons of this particular property?
- What does this weird clause in my agent's contract mean?
- Is this crack in the foundation a big deal, or just normal settlement?
- The seller just asked me why I can't get my own financing

what the heck do I say?

- The buyer wants to pay my wholesale fee in 6 months—what do I do?

And you know what ends up happening? You either:

- Don't make the offer at all, because you're afraid of making a mistake or
- Make the wrong offer, because you weren't able to evaluate ALL of the pros, cons, ins, and outs of the deal right up front.

You Need Expert Support to Do Deals, Period.

Ask yourself this:

"How much more successful would I ALREADY be if I'd had an expert—preferably a 6' tall redhead with 25 years' experience—that I could call on to help me evaluate deals, weigh out the pros and cons of strategies, and kick my butt when I needed it?"

If you're being honest with yourself, I bet your answer is, "A WHOLE lot more successful."

I've watched literally thousands of new real estate investors succeed and fail—and I can tell you that for those who actually make it in thus business, this kind of expert assistance is absolutely crucial.

In fact, I had a mentor when I was starting out in real estate and at every stage since. That's the God's honest truth, and if I hadn't had this help, I don't know how I would have done the 800+ deals that I have in my career.

I was just as scared and confused as you are at every step of the way—from making my first offer to wholesaling my first deal—and without the coaching of my various mentors, I'd probably have given up and become a corporate drone.

I Know—Expert Help is Hard to Find.

That's Why I Started the Inner Circle Program:

To Give You The Ongoing Support, Encouragement,

and Education You Need...At a Price You Can Afford!

I enjoy helping new investors like you get your first profi check—and helping you get from there to building an actual real estate business that creates both active and passive income for your family for generations.

Getting you to that next level is fulfilling for me—it is, in a wa , my real calling.

That's why I created the Real Estate Estate Goddess's Inner Circle—an affordable, pay-as-you-go program to get you the help you need to get where you want to go.

Look at All You Get for Just $39.97/Month:

1. **Unlimited e-mail coaching from me, personally.** The unlimited email coaching is the most important benefit of your Inner Circle membership. You can ask questions about specific deals, the real estate market in general, your goals and business plan, marketing—anything. As an Inner Circle member, you'll get a special email address to contact me—and quick answers to your real estate conundrums!

   And let me be clear: it's actually ME who will be answering your questions. It won't be some minion, or a dude in a phone room in Utah. It will be me, personally, as long as you're a member.

2. **A weekly "Inner Circle-only" e-lesson** with news about the real estate market, links to free resources, questions and answers from your fellow Inner Circle members, and success stories from real-life investors. This e-lesson covers more advanced topics than my Tuesday "REGoddess E-letter", which you can also choose to continue to receive. Recent topics have included how to develop your marketing, how to negotiate with

sellers, how to control contractors, real estate ethics, how to find buyers for wholesale deals, and how to form a mastermind group.

3. **A weekly no-sales web class series that teaches you all the fundamentals of real estate investing.** Each Wednesday night at 8 p.m. EST, you'll get a different 50-90 minute lesson on important topics ranging from how to evaluate properties to how to find great deals to how to wholesale, retail, landlord, choose an entity, make a business plan, and more! You'll learn 3 ways to buy properties without banks how to negotiate with sellers, how to use contracts—it's a complete education in the important basics of real estate education, and it's FREE with your Inner Circle membership!

4. **At least 10% off all of my homestudy courses and events.** Want to go even further in learning about a particular topic such as wholesaling, marketing, creative finance, negotiation or business building? I've got a course for that.

    And as an Inner Circle member, you're entitled to a standard discount of 10% off of all of my already-inexpensive homestudy courses and bootcamps.

5. **Special "Inner Circle Only" events at many of my live seminars and conferences.** Events like VIP cocktail parties with the speakers, free luncheons…whatever my creative brain can come up with as a special benefit for you

Your monthly investment in the Real Estate Goddess's Inner Circle is LESS than what you pay for cable TV—and a whole lot more likely to make you rich. At just $39.97 a month for all this education and support, it's a no-brainer.

But Wait, There's More—

Mention This Book When You Register, and

Get Your 1st Month for Just $1…

Yeah, I admit it…I'm trying to get you hooked.

And when you join for 1 month for just $1, and see the direct benefits to your confidence, your knowledge, and your bottom line, I know you will be.

That's why you'll want to continue for $39.97/month—so it's my job to convince you in 30 days that this program is worth a whole lot more than that, because, remember, you can cancel at any time.

And to make it even more of a no-brainer, you'll also get…
My Exclusive
Real Estate Business Plan Blueprint (a $99 value)
ABSOLUTELY FREE…

I'm going help you get started right with something you've never seen before: a business plan template that I've painstakingly developed JUST for real estate entrepreneurs. (Think I'm kidding? Go ahead—just TRY to find a business plan for real estate investors on the internet. Seriously. I'll wait. See what I mean?) This blueprint will guide you through the process of researching your own market, strategy, and business, and help you set smart, achievable goals for the next 1-5 years.

Not only will this step-by-step template launch you light-years ahead in your business—it will also impress the heck out of potential lenders and partners, and put you head and shoulders above your "competition" when you set out to raise money!

So let's summarize:

1. Join the Inner Circle today for $1
2. Get the expert help you need to do smart, profitable deal
3. Get the education you need to make money fast
4. Get the business plan blueprint you need to plan your strategy and impress potential money people (limited time only)
5. Quit whenever you like!

I Think That's What They Call a No-Brainer.
So Go to REGoddess.com Right Now to Join,
Or Call 888-275-8362

Geez, this is so good, even I want to join.

So don't wait—risk a few bucks and get the best, most affordable training and support you'll ever see.

I look forward to working with you!

Vena Jones-Cox

Host, Real Life Real Estate Investing

WMKV radio

Made in the USA
Monee, IL
24 November 2021

82944970R00066